Free Bird

A Memoir

AMBER WHITE

Adam and I spread Dad's ashes "on ground we liked." I couldn't part with all of him and kept two handfuls of his remains, which found their way to the cover of this book. I think this would have been Dad's favorite resting place. Front and center…forever immortalized.

Very special thanks to Jill Peterson Photography for cover photography.

For you dad,
But mostly for me

ACKNOWLEDGMENTS

First, I'd like to thank myself for taking the time to understand my feelings, put them to paper, and share them with the world. In this project I have found myself and learned that love and acceptance need only come from within. To my loving husband Dean and my children, Conner and Carson: thank you for believing in me when my belief faltered. You have been a constant in my life, and your love and encouragement keep me inspired. Loving thanks to my beautiful mother, Joyce and my brilliant brother, Adam. This is not *my* story, it is *ours* and your support has meant the world to me. To my best friend, Becky Cortese, who has been instrumental in keeping me focused on my true mission here on earth. You, like all other good things in my life, are not here by coincidence. You are "true light and love" and your unearthly insight is a powerful gift to the world. So many other family and friends have helped me. They took the time to either read my story, offer advice, and/or provide encouragement: Debra Collins, Brandon Collins, Addison Collins, Julie Hahn, Tiffany Ross, Heather Schon, Kelly Legnon, Bryan Wagstaff, Denise Vega, Yolanda Martinez-Monteon, Sylvia Sanchez, Laura McMahon, Cheryl Green, Cathy McBeth, Jayme Brittingham, and Dr. Steve McLaughlin. I'd like to give special thanks to those on juvenile probation I've had the privilege of supervising. Please know that I have learned from you all. My sincerest hope is that you will someday learn to believe in and love yourself. There is no obstacle big enough to prevent you from achieving anything your human spirit sets out to do. When you know self-love, that is all you will need, and you will move mountains. Last, I would like to thank "My boss's boss." Your actions helped me discover my true mission here on earth. To love myself. *I* am the mission. *Sometimes, the most important messengers in your life are disguised as real assholes.*

CONTENTS

CHAPTER 1

"Kids, get in here!"

"Kids, get in here!" Dad yelled. Adam and I looked at each other with concern. Mom was the one who did the disciplining around the house…that is unless you did something *really* bad. We didn't wait for him to call us again. We ran straight to his bedroom. "Yes, Dad?"

"Get in here. I want you to see something." He yelled from his bathroom. Adam and I peered in and saw Dad standing there in his underwear. He motioned to the toilet and proclaimed, "Take a look at that!"

There was a huge crap in the toilet, so large that it reached itself entirely out of the water and sat there "dry-docked." Adam and I squealed in disgusted disbelief at the size of Dad's *Masterpiece*. Dad was as self-centered as they come. As far as he was concerned, even the shit he produced was a marvel worthy of observance and praise.

This is the story of my life:

When I was thirteen years old, I wrote Dad's first eulogy. I sat down and penned a heartfelt tribute and cried as if he were really gone. He hadn't actually died yet. Rather, he had just nearly killed himself. A part of me believed that grieving for Dad in advance would help prepare me for the inevitable. Odds were…Dad was not going to live long. I don't think he really wanted to anyway; he was a *free bird*.

Webster's Dictionary defines the word *Crazy: 1a. full of cracks or flaws, unsound; b. crooked, askew; 2a. mad, insane; b. impractical, erratic; c. being out of the ordinary: unusual; 3a. distracted with desire or excitement; b. absurdly fond; c. passionately preoccupied.* Yes, I think that sums him up. Dad was all of those things…maybe we all are to some degree.

I think it is safe to say that children have little perspective on what *crazy* actually is. That is to say…when you live with a crazy parent, you don't realize they are crazy. Crazy is the norm and by that rationale I guess that makes me a little crazy too. As a kid, I knew our family was different, but crazy? No way. *Crazy* is subjective, and the word carries a bad reputation. Suffice it to say, Dad was a special brand of crazy. The exciting, fun kind of crazy that decides to wake everyone up in the middle of the night to go and get pie or drive to Las Vegas.

Resilience, a strong set of coping skills, and Mom account for me surviving my early childhood. Don't get me wrong, I'm really glad I was born into a dysfunctional family *now* because it was downright character building. But in retrospect, it was rough at times and those who were witness to my life can attest to the fact that I am an anomaly, that is, a mutation not consistent with my given environment. There is no good reason I can conjure up to explain how I triumphed against all odds. Only perhaps to say that I had inherited an invaluable gene from Dad. He was an absolute fighter, and I was the most similar person to him on Earth.

I grew up in the 1970's in a California suburb not unlike many "normal" families. I lived with Mom, Dad, and Adam, my overachieving older brother. Adam was three years my senior. He was a handsome devil with blond hair and wise brown eyes. You would think being adorable was enough, but he also possessed above average intelligence. This made life hell for me because trying to keep up with him proved futile and frustrating. Adam was the golden child, and my parents were perpetually beaming with pride because of the perfect grades he brought home. To top it off, Adam was enrolled in special "MGM" curriculum. These were the classes set aside for the smart kids, and back then, schools made no effort to safeguard the "self-esteem" of all of us *average* students. Even the acronym was pompous and superior: "Mentally Gifted Minor." We dumb kids knew the "MGM" kids had more resources, better teachers, and a far superior curriculum, and it sucked. I referred to the program as "Mentally Gifted Morons" in defiant protest of my mediocrity.

Dad told me years later that a school psychologist contacted him to discuss Adam's admittance. He told Dad that students in the top 4% were admitted into "MGM" and Adam actually fell in the 7th percentile. The psychologist told Dad the committee believed a "domestic problem" accounted for Adam's lower score, and they indeed thought he was suitable for the program. Dad was the king of arrogance. His ego was huge, but also fragile. He certainly wasn't celebrating the news that the panel thought his son was gifted; all he heard was the other part....the condescending "domestic problem" part. He was beyond offended, and he told the man, "I'm an intelligent man. I know a knock when I hear one!" The psychologist countered, "Sir, can I ask you the difference between longitude and latitude?" Dad said, "Sure, one goes one way, and the other goes the other way." The psychologist replied, "That is exactly what your son said." Dad couldn't really argue with that logic and allowed Adam to be in the program. Adam blossomed, got even smarter than he already was, and his participation in "MGM" was an ever-present slap in the face for me. I hadn't even been invited to take the test to be a part of the program, so I figured that definitely made me dumb.

Adam had the first-born edge, he was male, and he was "gifted." These facts kept me in a constant state of inferiority. In addition, as far as I was concerned every person in my family was partial to Adam, including my grandparents. Mom's parents loved the fact that Adam played the trumpet, just like his grandpa, and Dad's parents had a special place for Adam because he was the only grandson out of their five grandchildren. In retrospect, my inferiority complex was likely a self-imposed illusion. But at the time I could see it no other way. I was the dumb one, the afterthought to Adam, and it felt wretchedly real.

Despite always feeling second best, I loved Adam and we got along pretty well. It wasn't his fault that he was smarter and sweeter. Adam was easy-going, unlike me. He had a vulnerable sensitivity about him and was mired down by an inner need to excel and please others. By nature, my brother was responsible and conscientious beyond his years, two traits he must have inherited from my mother. You never had to tell Adam to do his homework or clean his room. He just knew to do it. I think most of the time he provided more guidance to my parents than he received, and because of this he was treated like an adult by the time he was eight years old.

Adam was the type of kid who saved aluminum cans and put his birthday money in the bank. I was pretty oblivious to our family's dysfunction at the time, but Adam was keenly insightful. This had to make things infinitely harder for him. When I was around seven years old, I walked into Adam's room and found him crying. He wasn't in trouble, he hadn't done anything wrong. He had just found out that my parents drained his bank account to pay the utility bills. Adam had probably been saving that hundred forty-eight bucks half of his short life…and he had just been robbed. My parents reassured him that the money would be paid back in full, but Adam knew he would be in line after the other bill collectors. He wasn't going to see that money for a long time.

My mother was a gem of a woman. Her parenting style was rigid and militant, so I do recall contemplating many times whether or not she loved me. Mom was strong…the rock of the family. She had an overdeveloped set of morals and ethics and spent an inordinate amount of time imparting these lessons. She was responsible for rearing us kids properly, and that was no easy task considering her training was constantly being derailed by Dad. Mom ran a tight ship and cleaned at a furious rate. Our home's cleanliness and we kids were the only things she could control and control she did. I think she was trying to create some normalcy. A valiant attempt to rally order where chaos reigned. Try as she might to stave off utter confusion, her efforts were often futile because she had no control over Dad—no one did.

Dad was a rather short man, which I think in part generated his sassy nonconformist attitude. Despite his small stature, he possessed a powerful life force and a zealous charisma similar to the likes of Charles Manson or Jim Jones who served up a deadly drink to his followers. Okay, Dad wasn't that sinister (I don't think he ever killed anyone) but believe me I can say with confidence that he rivaled some of the most notorious individuals ever known.

Dad was a willful creature. He often said, "Make your own plans, or be at the mercy of those who make them for you." Rest assured that Dad was never at the mercy of someone else's design; he always had a plan and, in all likelihood, it involved using someone else to do his bidding. Dad was skilled at skirting responsibility and delegating tasks to others. He simply didn't do anything he didn't want to do. Most people complain and procrastinate when required to carry out certain difficult duties or obligations in life, but ultimately responsibility prevails, and they begrudgingly do what must be done. Dad didn't see it that way. He approached everything with a sense of *choice*. If he didn't want to do something and it needed to be done, he would simply find someone else to do it.

As far as Dad perceived it, he was the master of the universe. He didn't take kindly to others imposing their ideas or plans into his mission, and his mission was to *feel good*. If you were in his life, your mission would be the same-- to make him feel good. Simply put, Dad's five senses dictated his behavior. They were the vehicles that transported information to the pleasure center of his brain and made him feel good. His five senses were insatiable and superseded any vestiges of his conscience. Dad truly believed that if it felt good it couldn't be bad, and he was on a quest to discover what felt best so he could do it with gusto. Unfortunately, the things that felt best to Dad were either illegal, dangerous, or deadly.

Getting attention felt good, and Dad was most certainly an attention getter. He had absolutely no moral filter and loved to shock and offend others. When a thought popped into his head, he did not take a moment to consider how the recipient might receive the information. Honestly, I don't think he cared, because in his opinion he was delivering the truth and that was far more important than someone else's feelings. Dad loved to experience the impact he had on others and the world. He got a jolt of excitement each time his comments were met with a look of horror.

If you weren't sufficiently shocked by Dad at the onset, he'd go out of his way to indoctrinate you. I think he made it a point to test every person in his life, an initiation of sorts. He needed to gauge your threshold for abuse and determine how loyal you would be to him. You were either with him or against him. Those who accepted Dad completely were in his inner circle. A tough place to get, an even tougher place to be… subject to his consuming *will*.

Some who knew Dad as a teenager speculate that a car accident was responsible for making him *crazy*. I really like this excuse best. The fact that he had sustained brain damage was a foolproof excuse and imparted a respectable "I beat death" superhero quality. Indeed, Dad was hard to kill, and it was a darned good thing because had he not survived that car crash I would have never been born.

Dad was only nineteen years old when he and a friend decided to drive to Tijuana for some fun. On the way back home, Dad's buddy fell asleep at the wheel and they crashed head on into a ditch. Dad was taken to the hospital unconscious, and doctors told Grandma the bleak news. Dad sustained major head trauma which caused his brain to swell and created pressure within his skull. If left untreated, he would likely die. The doctors told Grandma that they needed to perform an emergency surgery to relieve the pressure on Dad's brain. I imagine medical science was still relatively crude in the 1960's, but something had to be done. There was little choice, so Grandma consented to the procedure, and the doctors drilled several holes in Dad's head to relieve the pressure on his brain. Afterwards he lay in a coma for two weeks dead to the world and Mom, his high school sweetheart, kept vigil at his bedside and waited for him to come back to her.

Mom was hopelessly in love with Dad. Not right in the beginning, but in short order Dad's oppressive *will* enslaved her. She met Dad at a high school dance. She was fifteen years old and Dad was seventeen. He was smitten with Mom and once he danced with her, he would allow no other boys an opportunity to do the same. The day after the dance, he went to her house to see her and when he learned she was not home, he waited there… for hours.

Mom said Dad was immediately pushy and possessive. He asked where she had been all day when she returned home, as if she already needed permission to go out. "I told you I was going surfing today" Mom told him, annoyed. But Dad's charm ultimately won her over. Mom said he looked just like James Dean and dressed like him as well: A greaser type who wore jeans and a white t-shirt rolled at the sleeve to hold his pack of cigarettes. *A rebel without a cause.*

Dad did finally wake from his coma. I think Mom's love brought him back. Aside from some initial forgetfulness and some occasional word confusion, the surgery didn't rob Dad of his faculties. He seemed to escape death rather unscathed. Mom told me that she didn't notice anything different about Dad's personality or behavior after the accident, but I don't think she was an objective judge of the before and after. She was blinded by love. I asked Grandma some years later if she noticed anything unusual about Dad after his car crash. Grandma couldn't recall anything unusual either, but she did tell me that weeks after the accident Dad kept seeing a bird fly through his bedroom. He would say, "There goes the bluebird of happiness" as he followed the imaginary thing with his finger. We'll never know for certain if those holes drilled into Dad's head changed him, made him crazy as some suspect, but I think something was shaken loose. Ultimately, Dad's accident was fortuitous. The Vietnam War was raging at the time, and when he went down to the draft board to take his medical exam with bandages over the holes bored through his head, they looked at him like he was crazy. Dad's essence was so powerful that I'm surprised he couldn't convince the medical examiners to send him off to war, bandaged head and all. He thought he was invincible and he lived accordingly, barging his way through life and telling destiny and caution: "Step aside, I know what I'm doing." He lived so fearlessly that I imagine he believed *he was indestructible*. Nothing seemed to frighten him; certainly, a foreign war was no different. In the end, the draft board told Dad, "Go home son." I'm pretty certain Dad left pissed off, believing they made a huge mistake. He didn't like failure, and rejection was particularly unimaginable, even when it was to his benefit.

Mom and Dad wanted to get married soon after the car accident, but Mom was still in high school and her folks insisted that she graduate before getting married. So, they waited a few months for Mom to finish school and right after graduation, they married in a church at "Rose Hills Memorial Park"… a cemetery! This foreboding irony should have served as a serious warning to Mom, but she was madly in love with Dad. A murder of crows could have descended on her and she would have remained steadfast in her dedication to Dad. But, for some reason, Dad waivered that day. Years later, he told Mom that he had had second thoughts as he stood at the altar. He told the pastor that he had "changed his mind" as Mom was walking down the aisle, and the pastor replied, "Too late now son, here comes your bride." Dad's admission devastated Mom…his honesty had no pity or sense. There was no doubt, Dad loved Mom. Why then, would he want to jeopardize the best thing that had ever happened to him? Maybe, deep down, he knew he would break Mom's heart and this was his attempt to head off the inevitable. Dad seemed to consistently reject the good in his life and this pattern confounded him.

Mom got a job at a telephone company after graduation and earned a small wage to put Dad through college. He eventually graduated with a bachelor's degree in business, and he found a job selling business forms. He was a born salesman, a likable con. He quickly built good relationships with his customers, and they loved him. Dad really did have a knack for gaining people's trust. There was a gritty genuineness to him…an honesty even they could not deny. He wasn't a cheesy salesman who was going to sneak and lie to rob you of your money. But he did overcharge you for his services and tell you that he was "worth it." Then he would somehow justify himself so completely that you would thank him for fleecing you.

True to Dad's nonconformist style, he quickly realized that working for someone else was the pits. Certainly, it was only a matter of time before he would be fired for insubordination anyway. Within two years of Dad's new job, he formulated a plan to replicate his employer's business, essentially to steal it and go into business for himself. Dad dreamed big. Not only would he sell the business forms as he did before, he would print them as well. He had all the templates for the business forms and a fan base of loyal customers. All that he lacked were printing presses and some capital. Money was not going to stand in the way. Dad had his own personal bank, his "Mama Brown."

CHAPTER 2

Your daddy was like the "Pied Piper"

Your Dad was always spirited and charismatic. Even as a young boy he had no problem organizing mischief for the neighborhood kids. They followed him like the "Pied Piper." When he was about ten or so, he went outside with his bow and arrow and a crowd of kids convened around him. He aimed the arrow into the sky and sent it into space. Your daddy quickly realized the arrow was bound to come back down and he yelled to the crowd, "Get out of the way, run!" The kids scattered and your daddy stood a while looking into the heavens, probably deciding whether he wanted to play chicken with that arrow. When he finally made a dash for it, that arrow came racing down to find him and struck him squarely atop his head. I just about died when he walked in the door. Blood had run completely down his face. I couldn't even make him out!

-Mama Brown

Mama Brown, Dad's mom, was a special woman. I knew Mama Brown simply as Grandma, and that is what I called her. Dad always called her Mama and when he was talking to me about her, he never referred to her as Grandma, always Mama Brown. Mama Brown was born on March 5th, which also happens to be my birthday, and this commonality bonded us in a unique and special way. She was enthusiastically optimistic. Nothing brought her down. She always saw the upside to any situation, and true to her Pisces sign she, too, was a dreamer.

Mama Brown was a wise woman, a social worker by profession, with a kind heart and common sense on all matters, except for those involving Dad. As insightful as she was, she had inadvertently created a monster. Dad pretty much ran the show from the time he was old enough to conjure up a bad thought, and he was constantly getting into mischief. He took Mama Brown's Plymouth once when he was fourteen years old. He couldn't even see over the wheel, and he ended up crashing it into a church.

Mama Brown spoiled Dad terribly, which in turn created his attitude of righteous entitlement. She "*had Dad's back*" and with her, there was no way he could fail or experience the consequences related to failure for that matter. Dad was never afraid to take risks, financial or otherwise, because the burdens of his failures were always carried by someone other than himself, namely, Mama Brown.

Mama Brown was a "Depression Baby" raised by her mother, my Great Granny Huff. Granny Huff was wily and survived the Depression by scrimping and finagling. Mama Brown told me that she never went hungry because they had a chicken farm, plus apple trees grew in her yard. Despite having many wonderful apples to eat from the trees in her yard, Mama Brown said she never enjoyed a good apple because Granny always made her eat the ones that were going bad first. Mama Brown's real daddy abandoned the family when she was four years old. All he left was a dollar in the bank account and a note to Granny that said she "Wasn't a good pal." Granny seemed to get along just fine without her husband. She was resourceful and sent Mama Brown door to door to sell eggs from their farm. Hard work and frugality were qualities indelibly stamped into Mama Brown. They were part of her character and would prove to shape her outlook for the rest of her days. She was perfectly fine with sacrifice; she was used to it. Her optimism made her highly adaptive, and the fruits of her hard work made her happy and always overshadowed the hardship.

Granny Huff, I am told, was a rather selfish woman who hoarded everything long after the Depression had ended. She had an affinity for procuring material goods, and what she did not acquire legitimately, she stole. She didn't need the stuff she stole; I suppose she just craved it. I remember visiting Granny a few times when I was a kid. Her house was so jam packed full of miscellaneous knick-knacks that I wanted to capture video footage to show my friends....*Nobody would believe the amount of crap she had amassed*, I thought.

Granny Huff had stuff stacked to the ceiling. There were so many boxes that they closed off the room, leaving only a single pathway, a maze that snaked its way through the length of the house. She had boxes and boxes of silverware and dozens of salt and pepper shakers that she had stolen from various restaurants. She also had a box of gentlemen's wallets. I remember looking through the box as a child, wondering why those men left their identification in their wallets before giving them to Granny. She was indeed a full-fledged kleptomaniac. Mama Brown told me that when she was a little girl, Granny Huff would take her to the department store to buy a dress but would scam the merchant by layering the dresses one on top of the other in the dressing room. She would then proceed to the register with Mama Brown still wearing the garments and proclaim, "We'll take this one and my daughter would like to wear it out of the store." Then they would walk right out, paying only for the dress on top- shoplifting the dresses hidden beneath.

Granny Huff was something else…every holiday, she'd tell me and the other great grandchildren that she put money in our very own special bank accounts. This went on for years. You would figure that for Christmas, Easter, birthdays, and everything in between, this money would have really accumulated. But none of us ever saw a penny. I've been told, Granny took all that money to the horse track and gambled it. None of us kids were old or bold enough to ever ask for it. This pissed Dad off to no end. I don't think he ever forgave her for lying to us kids. Granny Huff lived like a pauper but was a millionaire. When she died, they found thousands and thousands of dollars hidden throughout her house. She had so many bank accounts, she could no longer keep track of them all, and Mama Brown had a heck of a time accounting for all the hidden assets. Besides the cash Granny Huff squirreled away, she had also managed to amass ten rental properties. I guess you could say she was the master of all cons and quite possibly the carrier of the shitty gene that skipped a generation and landed soundly in Dad.

Granny Huff should receive credit for one notable accomplishment; that is paying off Mama Brown's first husband (Dad's real father) to leave and never come back. Mama Brown was newly married. Dad must have only been one or two years old at the time. On that fateful day, Mama Brown's husband had given her $10.00 to purchase a pair of high-heeled shoes. Resourceful as she was, she found a pair on sale for $2.50. She used the remainder of the money to purchase a couple of other personal items, believing the $10.00 was hers to spend.

When her husband learned that the shoes cost only $2.50 and the change from the $10.00 had not been returned, he flew into a rage. He cornered her and used that new shoe to hammer her head. Every clobbering blow sent her further toward the ground, like he was driving in a nail. Granny Huff heard Mama Brown's screams, and she came running to the rescue. "You obviously are not happy here, why don't you just leave!" Granny yelled. "Well, if I had that motorcycle I've been wanting, I would leave!" he countered. "How much does that motorcycle cost?" Granny inquired. "$275.00" He replied.

Granny Huff then offered him a deal that would change Mama Brown's future forever. "I'll give you the money for that motorcycle, in exchange for you leaving on it…for good." Mama Brown's husband, my Dad's real daddy, took the deal and never came back. He abandoned his entire family for a $275.00 motorcycle.

Mama Brown landed on her feet and met a sailor named Cecil who had just returned from war. She married him a short time later, and he raised my Dad and his brother as though they were his own children. Mama Brown told me that she and Grandpa tried for many years to have a child together, with no success. When she went to the doctor to discover why she could not get pregnant, they found cancer in her uterus. The doctors were able to remove the cancer, which was isolated and had not yet spread through her body. Grandma viewed things differently after that. Her optimism turned to exuberance. Life was precious, and she was abundantly fortunate. She took nothing for granted and found wonder and enjoyment in every small thing she undertook. The way she saw it, her first husband, Dad's real dad, had served his purpose. He had provided two beautiful children, Dad and his older brother, and probably saved her life. Grandma probably would have never discovered the cancer in its early stages if she had remained married to her first husband.

If there was one thing Granny Huff imparted to Mama Brown, it was resourcefulness and frugality. The ability to make eleven cents out of a dime. Because of this, Mama Brown was in good financial shape and her purse strings were tight unless Dad was asking for the dough. When Dad asked Mama Brown for the startup money to open his printing business, she forked over the cash with little hesitation; and *Dino's Printing* was born.

Dad had never operated a printing press in his life, but this hardly put a damper on his grandiose plan. He found an industrial building, bought up several huge printing presses, and made up the most fabulous business cards the world had ever seen. These were no ordinary business cards. They were printed on beautiful multi-colored see-through plastic cards emblazoned with "Dino's Printing" in gold lettering.

His business cards, I would find, were at the crux of Dad's reality. If he had a business card saying it was so, it created a demonstrable existence that he totally believed in… despite its real truth. He could have printed up a card representing himself as a doctor or lawyer and he most certainly would have believed in its tangibility, at least enough to absolutely fool others, possibly even a polygraph. Dad really bought into the reality of the business card; having a card this special served to bolster his already inflated ego.

Dad was no dummy. He needed a workhorse to sustain his operation. He had the ideal candidate at his disposal and he didn't even have to pay her- my Mom. Mom told me years later that she would work for weeks on a huge job, laboring and stressing to meet a deadline. At the end, when she had finished the job, Dad would give her a $20.00 bill and say, "Great job, go buy yourself something nice." Mom allowed this type of treatment and it defined her value...*worthless.* She learned to run the presses in no time and was better at it than Dad. While Mom did the heavy labor, Dad secured new accounts. Mom often complained that Dad wasted time at the neighbor's house drinking coffee and smoking cigarettes instead of drumming up business, but he seemed to bring in a steady stream of orders.

I remember going to Dad's print shop a couple of times. I was about four or five years old, and I found it boring. Mom would always have me bring a few toys and then tell me that I needed to play and not bother them while they worked. I liked the way the print shop smelled of chemicals, coffee, and glue. There was a big drafting table in one area with pencils, erasers, Dad's fabulous business cards, and razor blades, but Mom always told me not to make a mess or touch anything.

I was fascinated by all those razors attached to long metal holders. Mom told me repeatedly not to touch them because they were very sharp. They didn't look that sharp since they were so small. I doubted Mom and wondered, how sharp is *very sharp*? I took the razor and held it in my small hand. Then I dragged it lightly across the fatty part of my thumb. It wasn't that sharp; it hadn't cut me at all. I dragged it along my thumb a second time with a little bit more pressure and again, no cut. *Mom was wrong,* I thought. The third time I ran it across my thumb, blood poured out of the gash. Mom seemed angry rather than concerned about my wound. I thought I was going to get a spanking to go along with my injured thumb.

Despite our industrial-sized printing shop, Dad seemed to conduct most business deals at home in his office...which incidentally served as my brother's bedroom. Poor Adam... when Dad was working, he would shut the door and emerge hours later allowing the smoke to waft out in a billowing mass. If you dared to open the door to go inside, you could cut the smoke with a knife. Adam's bedroom was quite literally one giant ashtray. I think Adam was addicted to cigarettes long before he turned sixteen years old and began smoking.

CHAPTER 3

Mom liked to "rough it"

We were in Yucca Valley, one of the hottest parts of California, somewhere in the Mohave Desert. I must have been four or five years old. Dad drove us in the big silver truck to visit Mom's cousins. We were traveling down the road when a huge snake crawled through a gap in the engine lid and slithered up the window. We all screamed and begged Dad to turn the windshield wipers on to throw the thing off, but he wouldn't. Dad pulled the truck to the side of the road, got out, and snatched the thing up like a snake handler. Then he wrapped that snake around his neck, got back behind the wheel, and set off driving again. We all screamed like crazy as Dad played it up, flailing his arms and legs acting as if the snake had squeezed too tightly and cut off his air flow. As much as we wanted that snake out of the car, we were hypnotized by the "Dad Show." Dad was the conqueror of all things, beasts included. He would release the snake only after it submitted to his tricks, and of course it did.

Dad played by his own rules. He was an island and didn't need permission from anyone for anything. Because he was cocky with little impulse control and a wad of cash that the business brought in, he did what felt good, and buying toys for himself felt good. He bought a boat when I was four years old. As with any other large unnecessary purchase, he didn't bother consulting Mom. He just came home towing that monstrosity behind our big silver Chevy. Mom really was the most accommodating and forgiving woman on the face of the planet. Initially, she put up a fuss and scolded Dad for his impulsiveness, but he could talk her into anything. Ultimately, Mom embraced most all of Dad's hare-brained ideas and schemes. Not only because she loved him but because she was powerless against him.

I'll hand it to him…Dad was exciting and spontaneous. After he brought that boat home, his charisma and adventurous attitude incited the neighbors just as it did us kids. Within a year of Dad's boat purchase, three of our neighbors bought boats of their own and signed on to whatever expeditions were planned. Thanks to that boat, bonds were formed with people I will forever call my friends.

Our vacations always started out the same. Dad would pack our truck with supplies and luggage so haphazardly that objects would inevitably fly or bounce right out. Mom would holler and beg Dad to pull over to retrieve the item, but Dad saw no point. Mom and Dad would then sit in silence making that six-hour drive feel like forever. I think Dad packed the truck recklessly on purpose rather than just in haste in order to risk our goods and feel the thrill of the gamble.

Mom liked to camp out, and "roughing it" was the way she chose to live, not just for weekend camping trips but in general. She lived in a constant state of hypervigilance in her attempts to *survive* Dad's bizarre behavior. I don't think it ever dawned on her to put a stop to the chaos; she just buckled down and "roughed it." She adapted to her circumstances and mostly relinquished control of her destiny to Dad, like a dog who won't run away from a master who beats him. Granted, Dad never laid a hand on Mom; he didn't need to. His words were far more powerful than his hands and strangely, Mom really seemed to enjoy serving him. It gave her purpose, made her feel useful, and proved her strength. Mom really was tough. Dad knew it too, and he called her his "tree-climber." I would venture to guess that Mom's strength was in part why Dad chose her. He was exacting. Certainly, he saw Mom's exploitable characteristics as well. She had the perfect combination of resilience, servitude, and loyalty… it absolutely promised long-standing obedience.

Mom was perfectly content being the workhorse, and as soon as we pulled up to the camp site she would get to work. She knew exactly what needed to be done and would methodically clear an area of rocks and twigs in preparation for the tent. She'd unload the contents of the truck and erect the tent virtually by herself while Dad drank a beer. Then just like at home, she would spend an hour sweeping and cleaning that musty thing out. Mom asked nothing of Dad, and he was more than happy to oblige.

Although we went to many different lakes and rivers, the Sacramento Delta remains the most memorable. For several years in a row, our family and a bunch of our neighbor friends caravanned there together and pitched in to rent a giant grassy property complete with its own small beach. The trees on the property seemed never ending and provided shade and entertainment. As a kid, I was certain these trees dropped their leaves just for me… because they enjoyed watching me run across the camp to catch them as they fell. Our camp was as big as a football field, although it probably just felt that way because I was so small. It was the most wonderful place I knew as a kid and probably the only thing I ever really looked forward to. That place was responsible for my best childhood memories.

Boat rides, sand castles, and soda pop were the order of the day. Even Mom seemed relaxed. Mom and Dad took turns water skiing several times a day behind the boat, and I got to hold the big orange flag when they fell. Dad went nuts on a single ski. He flew across the wake and leaned from side to side, creating a giant wall of spray that shot out from under his ski. When he was tired of skiing, he'd signal with his hand to drop him back off at camp. The boat would zip back toward the shore line and Dad would lean outside of the wake. Then he'd let go of the rope at precisely the right moment, allowing him to glide right onto the beach.

When I was about five, Dad put some skis on me and threw me out in the water. "Just hold on to the rope Am, you can do it!" He yelled. I very much wanted to please Dad; I would have jumped off a cliff if he told me to. I just wanted him to love me. The boat took off and I dragged behind it for a long time, never mounting the water on those skis. I held on even as water went into my mouth and nose and when I thought I might drown, I finally released the rope's handle. I coughed and spit up water, crying as my little body bobbed around in the water. Unconcerned, Dad scooped me back into the boat and said, "Why did you keep hanging on? You were really dragging back there!" Dad never told me to let go of the rope; he was never big on instructions.

Our trips didn't always go smoothly. Dad's impulsiveness was always the cause of routine chaos. Adam was just a baby when Dad crashed the gold Chevy Camaro on the way to the Salton Sea, near California's Coachella Valley. He hit a truck that was stopped in his lane while going full speed. Mom's head broke the windshield. They found her in a heap in the foot compartment of the vehicle, and the passenger side was completely smashed in. They say that if Mom had been wearing her seat belt, she would have been decapitated. When she woke up, she was in the hospital and doctors were stitching up her face.

"Don't worry honey, we can get you plastic surgery." Dad said reassuringly.

"What? What happed?"

"We got into a car accident, but everyone is okay."

"What about the car?" Mom asked.

"Awe, don't worry about that car, the ashtray was full anyway." Dad responded.

CHAPTER 4

Dad's favorite sport– fighting with strangers

"What are you putting on your lawn Chuck?" Dad asked. "Just some fertilizer" Chuck responded. "Oh, you don't want to put that type on your lawn…mushrooms love it. You'll have em' everywhere." "Awe, Bullshit Dean!" Chuck responded.

Later that day, Dad went to the store and bought cartons of mushrooms. Then he crept over to Chuck's in the middle of the night and blanketed his entire lawn with those spores. I wish I could have seen Chuck's face that next morning. Dad's playfulness was endearing. I suspect that is why Chuck loved him so much.

My parents met Chuck and his wife DeeDee in 1971, before I was born. They bought brand new track homes across the street from one another in Cerritos and became fast friends. DeeDee had long beautiful brown hair and a sweet disposition. She loved to talk and shop and dragged Mom to Sears whenever possible. Dad spent most mornings at Chuck's house drinking coffee and smoking cigarettes. DeeDee said Dad would come over at six o'clock in the morning and bang on their bedroom window to wake them up. DeeDee would tell Dad, "Just give me a minute Dean, I'll put some coffee on." Chuck and DeeDee always felt like family to me. In fact, when I was born they were there at the hospital to welcome me into this world. Dad said he took one look at me, then looked at Chuck suspiciously and said jokingly, "Hey, she looks just like you Chuck!" About eleven months after I was born, Chuck and DeeDee had a little girl of their own, Becky. She became my best friend, my soul sister.

Becky and I were constant playmates. We shared a powerful bond that proved to withstand distance and time. We had tea parties, played house, danced, and sang. When Becky and I weren't together, I would stand at the curb and yell out to her over and over. Sometimes she would hear me and come out to the curb. Since we were not yet allowed to cross the street alone, we would stretch our arms out to one another from a distance. I loved Becky entirely. She was my sister and her dad Chuck…was the father I would have liked to have.

Chuck was a tall, burly man with a contagious laugh. Full of life and love, he hugged and doted on me like I was his own. When I hugged him, I could never reach all the way around, but I tried because I loved him so completely. Chuck was an admirable father and an all-around dynamic man. His display of affection for his only child, Becky, was like none I had ever seen, let alone experienced. He often came home with little surprises for Becky. Silly things like Tic-Tacs or a pack of gum. He cared, and his thoughtful, loving gestures were foreign to me. Dad didn't do those things for me. I longed for a father like Chuck and felt a close attachment to him. He was an insightful man. I imagine he knew I needed him for that purpose and was more than willing to oblige. He often gave me the loving attention I needed.

Spending time with Becky's family served as a constant reminder of what I didn't have. I was jealous, no doubt, but believed I was a special part of Becky's family and it felt good. Becky, ever generous, was perfectly willing to share her daddy with me, just as she shared everything else. *The universe has a special way of filling the voids.* Dad adored Chuck as much as I did, and Chuck proved to be one of the only humans capable of buffering Dad. Dad respected him.

When I was five years old, we were at McDonalds with Becky and her family when Dad got into a fight with a stranger in the parking lot. Dad and Chuck were making fun of the guy's "Jordache" jeans inside the restaurant. They mocked him for wearing girly jeans and referred to his fashion choice as "Big Bird Pants." I have no idea what the comment was supposed to mean, or why such a childish remark angered the man so much. But he was beyond offended and wanted a piece of Dad.

By the time we got out to the parking lot, all hell broke loose. Dad had just started taking *Kempo* karate classes and although he was a foot smaller than the guy, he was absolutely ready for battle. Dad's arrogance was intimidating. He bounced around the parking lot like a boxer and performed an impressive show of punches and kicks, letting that guy know what he was in for. I imagine Dad had been eagerly waiting for some sorry victim, so he could practice his new karate skills. He had probably instigated the fight for that reason alone. Mom was screaming the whole time, "Dean, not in front of the kids. Stop it!" I was scared, not for Dad but for the big guy coming after him. He had no idea who he was messing with. Dad never got to unleash on the guy who wore the *Jordache* jeans. Somehow, Chuck was able to mediate the altercation while Mom quickly ushered us kids to the car.

Over the years I'd come to learn that fighting with strangers was a particularly enjoyable hobby of Dad's, a sport he sought out. Unfortunately, Chuck wasn't always there to be the voice of reason. Dad's unruly behavior provided him plenty of opportunity to squabble with others; however, these occasions proved most contentious when Dad was behind the wheel. Long before the term "Road Rage" was coined, Dad invented the sport. He carried a gun in the glove compartment of the car. I'm not sure if it was his BB gun or something deadlier, but when people pissed him off while he was driving he simply reached over, grabbed the gun, and aimed it right at them. He did this a couple of times with the entire family in the car, scaring the shit out of us and the poor sap who "didn't know how to fucking drive."

Dad taking aim with his gun would have sufficed to fill the boldest person with terror, but that wasn't enough. He would roll down the window and wave the gun around wildly while he screamed obscenities and chased them down. Tailgaters got off easy. They were behind us and usually just got the abrupt brake lights as a consequence. It didn't matter if we were on surface streets or the freeway. If Dad was being followed too closely, he'd slam on the brakes with both feet using enough force to lift his ass clear off the seat. Our car came screeching to a halt on several different occasions. Surprisingly, we were never struck from behind and thank God for that... I can only imagine what Dad would have done in that instance. Dad's recklessness knew no bounds. He crashed every vehicle he ever owned.

CHAPTER 5

"Do as I say, not as I do"

-Dad's Credo

I awoke to fireworks exploding in my room, giant bursts of color all around me. I didn't know if I was awake or dreaming, but I was scared and ran to Mom and Dad's room crying. I was sweaty, but cold. Something was wrong. "Dean, she is burning up!" Mom yelled. The doctor said it was pneumonia. I was five years old.

I was a real needy, shy kid at that age. Mom didn't send me off to preschool, so I was attached to her like an appendage. She was dependable, the only constant. Being anywhere without Mom was anxiety provoking, so being left at the hospital alone was terrifying. They put a thick plastic tent around my bed. I thought it was to keep others from catching what I had. The nurses fought to keep my temperature down. They gave me cold baths and enemas daily, but my lungs remained full of thick mucus I could not expel.

I only remember one visitor, Mom's brother, Uncle Ed. He was a Vietnam veteran, a real bad ass. He stood there peering through my plastic tent, and he started to cry. He told me he loved me and then left, barely able to hold it together. His emotional response left me feeling frightened… *if he is scared and crying, I must be in real trouble*, I thought.

I remained in the hospital for a week before being discharged, but once home, I immediately relapsed. My fevers returned, and I threw up from coughing so violently. Every night Mom came into my room to pound on my back. She cupped her hands and then pounded away for about twenty minutes. She thought that would loosen up the phlegm in my lungs, so I could better cough that bitter goop up. But I didn't want it to come out. I was much more important with it inside, and everyone doting on me made me feel loved. I wanted to stay sick and made very little effort to cough that phlegm out to clear my lungs. I finally did get better. Apparently, like Dad, I too was hard to kill.

My brush with death toughened me up a little and kindergarten put some separation between me and Mom. I was scared and cried when Mom dropped me off the first day of school. I truly feared she would not come back for me. For some reason, I always felt like an afterthought… an inconsequential object that would be forgotten and swallowed up by the world. Life's harsher realities were beginning to emerge; however, these little hurdles were nothing compared to what Dad had in store for me. Dad's outrageous "reality-based training" was unsuitable for any child. He wasn't interested in the daily rearing of us kids; he left that to Mom. I think Dad just got a kick out of creating obstacles to harden and prepare me and Adam for life's adversities. I dare say Dad was entertained watching us fumble through life. He believed things could only truly be learned by experiencing them, and he didn't want to spoil any of life's shitty surprises.

Dino's Printing shop was doing quite well, and over the years it seemed to bring in a fairly consistent flow of cash. This seemed to satisfy Mom, but stability was not important to Dad; it bored him. As far as he was concerned, he had conquered the printing business, and it had lost its appeal. Dad seemed to suffer from a constant void in his life. A void that proved to be fickle, purposeless, and unidentified. He was never satisfied and seemed always on a mission to find something that *felt better*.

Dad spent less and less time securing accounts, and his presence at the print shop became sparse. He filled up his days drinking beer, smoking cigarettes, and contemplating life with his friends. One of Dad's friends happened to hold a job in the aerospace industry building military planes and space shuttles for the United States government. Dad was intrigued by the industry and wanted to know everything about it, so he arranged meetings with his friend at the local watering hole and they talked for hours about "jig and fixture" and the aerospace tooling process. Dad decided right there at that bar that he too would build fighter planes and space shuttles. I don't know what made him believe that he could break into this business with nothing more than the knowledge gained during his barroom chats, but I imagine it was the same special something that made him so wildly charismatic. Dad wasn't afraid to try anything. He possessed an unparalleled audaciousness that drew others to him like a magnet. He hatched dreams so grand and believed in their attainability so fully that you couldn't help but think his crazy plan was plausible. I never questioned Dad's potential. He seemed to do everything he set out to do and told me I could do the same....*anything*.

Dad wasted no time. He immediately got to work fabricating a resume detailing his vast knowledge and expertise in the aerospace industry; all absolute lies. I watched him work methodically at his drafting table. He looked like a mad scientist, sketching and cutting with the magic wand that held the sharp razor blade. Dad had a plan, as usual, and his plans always seemed to pan out. He used his printing press to create an extraordinary resume, something uncommon in the early 1980's since most people only had access to typewriters. Dad's creation was impressive and showy. The *piece de resistance* was the military plane gracing the background of that thick expensive paper. It absolutely promised him the job.

Dad was the world's greatest pretender, and his irrational confidence to pull off the impossible was nervy and intimidating. It was as if he actually believed his own lies, and he made others believers too. Dad didn't need that aerospace job; he owned his own business, so certainly he went into that interview feeling very cocky. There is no doubt in my mind that he came across as fearless and inspiring...and he was hired. Mom was surprised as anyone to learn Dad had a "Top Security" clearance and was now going to be building fighter planes for the military. But she always had an unreasonable faith in Dad and picked up the slack at the printing shop.

Dad was cunning. He sought out key people he could use to teach him the job. He never showed all his cards or let on that he knew nothing. He just asked for help in wily ways, ways that would not reveal his absolute ignorance. Dad was likable, and he quickly made friends who could be trusted with "stupid questions." Eventually, some of Dad's new friends discovered he was a fraud. But instead of outing him, they showed him the ropes and covered for him when he messed things up.

Aside from a couple of embarrassing moments, Dad learned the trade at a feverish rate. He possessed a new-found fervor for life and was filled with a manic zeal. I don't know what excited him more, learning a new trade or knowing he had pulled off the biggest scam of his life. He delighted in the fact that he had completely fooled the system. Not just any system, one that carried a "Top Security" clearance.

Dad all but abandoned the printing business. Mom struggled to run the shop alone, but she had become more and more fatigued. Dad's business had to be sold and soon after coming to this conclusion, it was. I was about seven years old when my folks said goodbye to "Dino's." At the time, I don't think Dad realized or appreciated the magnitude of his successful shop. He cast it aside in haste, like many good things. I think this is why he lived in a perpetual state of dissatisfaction. He was frustrated chasing his past, trying to duplicate or better what he had tossed away, and it was never as good the second time around.

CHAPTER 6

Sink or Swim

Memories are like a tapestry, a complex blueprint of interlacing threads. Some threads are seen, while others, equally important to the design, lie hidden beneath. I think this was God's plan…some memories remain hidden because they are simply better forgotten.

Childhood years felt long. It was a space filled mostly with boredom and solitude but peppered with Dad's entertaining volatility. Neither of my parents seemed interested in entertaining us kids, and I don't remember much "family time." Come to think of it, apart from our yearly camping trip to the Delta, I recall very few family outings. We lived twenty minutes from two theme parks, but the handful of times we went it was Mom who took us. We went to the occasional movie or park, but Dad certainly wasn't there. We never ate out at restaurants as a family. We didn't have the money.

Dad seemed to spend his time doing whatever he pleased, and Mom seemed to spend most of her time cleaning and working. I spent a good chunk of my time exploring the outdoors on my bike or skateboard. Mom would always whistle when it was time to come in for dinner, and that sound could be heard three or four blocks away. She'd place both pinkies in her mouth and when she blew, a piercing sound escaped...*BEEOOOOEEEEP!* Her whistle was powerful and unexpected coming from her petite frame. In my mind, it elevated her into a pretty special category. No one else's mom on the street could whistle like that, only the dads. Mom was a strange dichotomy. A combination of dominance and complete submissiveness. She was quite the force when she wasn't surrendering control to Dad. She had to be. She was virtually alone in her task of raising us kids and running the household.

Saturday was cleaning day at my house, a day of house and yard work. *I hated Saturdays.* Aside from cartoons in the morning, the day was going to suck. My list of chores could easily consume half the day, or so it felt, and Mom was never satisfied with the quality of my work. I particularly hated the yard work. We had a giant Ficus tree in the backyard that dropped thousands of tiny seed balls, and I was required to rake them up.

Being under that tree with the rake made me want to jump out of my skin. Bugs and spiders crept around and fled from the piles I raked. I much preferred scooping the dog's poop to raking under that tree. It was actually fun slinging the poop over the backyard fence into the ditch. I'm not sure which of my parents thought it prudent to do away with our dog's waste in this fashion, but it was deemed totally acceptable. Over the years, many *shitty* things seemed to make their way into the ditch behind our house.

Adam was responsible for mowing the lawn, which really must have freaked the neighbors out at first. He couldn't see over the mower's handle when Dad assigned him the task. But over the years, he managed to maneuver that powerful machine like a pro. Sometimes, the mower didn't have any gas, and Dad would siphon some out of the car. When Adam was about twelve, he assigned that duty to him as well.

Adam was siphoning gas from the car with the garden hose that day when I was passing through the garage. Adam was no dummy; he knew the task at hand was dangerous at best, so he reassigned the job to me. I looked up to Adam. Any task he was good enough to privilege me with I was certainly going to undertake. Like Dad, Adam had a little salesman in him, and he made gas siphoning sound really fun. "Listen Am, all you have to do is take little sips from the hose until you feel the gas on the tip of your tongue. Once you taste gas, just put the hose in the gas can and fill-er-up!"

It sounded easy enough, so I got straight to work. I sipped and sipped and sipped some more. I sipped for what seemed an eternity and still no gas! I was really growing impatient and Adam had long abandoned his chore, leaving me there in the garage alone. Finally, I thought, "I'll take one big sip of air, which will save me a bunch of time." But the gasoline must have been right there at the end of the hose and when I inhaled that last hefty breath, gas raced down my throat in a fiery rage.

A hideous scream escaped my body, but the sound was foreign; it sounded nothing like my voice. I frantically ran into the house and headed for the bathroom sink. I shoved my whole face in the sink and gulped water right from the faucet, hoping to wash the pain down my throat. But it remained and my screams just kept coming, almost involuntarily. Mom ran to the bathroom and demanded I tell her what happened. But when I attempted to speak, I had no control of my vocal chords. Nothing came out but those grisly, terrified screams.

I gasped for air between screams, and finally the gasoline seemed to make its way through my esophagus and into the pit of my stomach. When I could breathe, I told Mom what happened in a strained crackly voice. I wasn't sure if this strange new voice was permanent damage caused by the petrol or if it was just a result of the screaming, but I felt positively wretched. My throat hurt, and my stomach felt oddly bloated.

Mom was furious when she found out Dad had us kids siphoning gas. Mom yelled, "Dean, don't you think we should take her to the hospital?" "No, she'll be fine. All she needs is a slice of bread and some milk." I thought the event was pretty serious, but figured Dad knew best. So, I drank my milk and ate my bread, then burped gasoline for hours.

Dad was an early bird and loved the morning hours. Sometimes on the weekends he would turn the radio on and dance. "Just call me angel of the morning, baby," he'd sing. Then he would skip from side to side and jump to click his heels together. Dad's good moods were contagious. I knew that if he woke up singing, it was going to be a good day.

Despite there being very little "family time," Dad kept things lively with his spontaneity. On a couple of occasions, he told all the neighborhood kids, "Go get your bathing suits, we are going to the pool!" Everyone squealed and scattered home to get their suits and towels. Then we jumped in the back of Dad's big silver truck. The community pool was a few blocks away, and Dad would drive like a madman with all us kids laughing and rolling around in the back.

Dad was just like one of us kids; those other parents were crazy to leave him in charge of their offspring. He'd make himself the center of attention by coming up with a game, or sometimes he'd climb the pillars onto the roof surrounding the pool and swan dive in. One year, Dad taught Eddie, one of the neighborhood kids, how to swim. Dad noticed that Eddie was staying in the shallow end and asked why he wasn't playing "Marco Polo" with the rest of the kids. When Dad found out Eddie didn't know how to swim he said, "We'll fix that!" He picked Eddie up and threw him right into the deep end. Eddie's body sunk then bobbed back up to the surface. His eyes were round like saucers and his arms flailed wildly. "Swim Eddie, swim!" Dad yelled. Eddie fought the water hard, slapping it with determination and finally made his way over to the side where he latched on. "Ya Buddy! You know how to swim now!" Dad hollered excitedly. *Dad's teaching methods were always a matter of sink or swim.*

Dad was friends with all the neighbors, even though he threw their children into the deep end of the pool. They loved him, and who could blame them? He was entertaining as hell. Dad was behind the planning of camping trips, neighborhood shenanigans, and my favorite-- block parties.

The neighbors on our street gathered almost every Fourth of July for a giant block party. The adults found creative ways to completely block off our street using a combination of vehicles, caution tape, and kid's toys. As far as I was concerned, this was the best part of the celebration. It allowed me to run wild and carefree through the street...something Mom never let me do.

Those barriers made our street special, and I was a part of that. Any sap traveling down our street who didn't belong there was either going to have to find an alternate route to get to the other side or join the party. Dad always offered them a beer and encouraged them to join in the fun before sending them back the other way.

Mom put a "Slip-N-Slide" out on the front lawn, which would inevitably draw all the kids to our house. Our lawn was long enough to accommodate that big yellow strip of plastic, plus it sloped slightly making for a good, fast ride. "Slip-N-Slide" seemed a harmless sport to the amateur, but I quickly learned it wasn't for sissies. Being hurled onto the sidewalk or into one of the metal sprinkler heads was a real possibility. Someone usually left crying.

I think I was around ten years old the year Dad got his hands on some illegal fireworks from Tijuana: a load of bottle rockets, firecrackers, and a giant bomb appropriately named "King Kong." We couldn't wait till it got dark and Dad had a shit-eating grin on his face all day. I think he was more excited than us kids. Come dusk, Dad paced around the backyard as he inspected "King Kong." The thing was monstrous, and he was clearly impressed. I pretended to be a newscaster reporting on the evenings special Fourth of July detonations. "Sir, how do you intend to safely light the fuse?" I asked Dad. "Well, after I light that thing, I plan to run like hell!" He replied. "Sir, when will the firework show begin? The crowd is waiting." "Soon…soon" Dad said, brushing me off to inspect a brick of firecrackers. I was giddy with excitement, everyone was.

As soon as it got dark, Dad was ready with the first bottle rocket. He swigged the last of his beer, then plopped the rocket into the empty bottle. Dad stood in the backyard and held the bottle toward the ditch behind our house. "Okay, here we go!" he yelled, as he lit the fuse. The thing shot out of the bottle like a missile and streaked the night sky with a burning light. "Ya buddy!" Dad yelled as he grabbed a brick of firecrackers and jumped our wooden backyard fence. Dad planned to detonate a good portion of the fireworks in the cement ditch behind the house. We all waited for the deafening noise to begin and were startled by the sounds of Dad's hands and feet hitting the fence as he scrambled back over into our yard. Just then, "BANG, BANG, BANG…" The firecrackers snapped on for an eternity, echoing back and forth off the sloped cement walls. Dad had that look on his face…the wild-eyed one that made him infectious and irresistible. He was *alive* and just being around him, despite the inherent danger, made you feel alive too.

I watched in awe as Dad turned the night sky alive and awakened the ditch. "King Kong" was the finale, and that brick-like bomb did not disappoint. It let out thunderous claps, similar to what I imagine a war zone might sound like. We were all still hooting in appreciation when the police helicopter arrived and began circling overhead. "Get in the house, hurry up, hurry up!" Dad screamed. We all scrambled for the door and as Dad ran in, he systematically turned off every light in the house. "Shhhhh, quiet" he called out, as if the helicopter might hear us. I hid, hoping the police would not find me when they came to arrest our family.

When the doorbell rang I thought I might pee my pants. *Oh shit! The police are here to arrest us!* Dad crept out from his hiding spot to the peep hole after the second ring and paused deciding whether he was going to open the door. I held my breath. *Don't open it…don't open it.* Dad went for the door knob and my heart sank.

"Hi Elmer…" Dad began. Elmer was the curmudgeonly old neighbor who lived three doors down. A man so meticulous and anal, he believed it prudent to mow his lawn every two days to keep its golf course look.

Thank god, it's just Elmer, I thought. But when I heard him lay into Dad, I reckoned Dad probably wished it had been the cops at our door instead. Apparently, one of Dad's bottle rockets had landed on Elmer's wood roof. The old man was required to get his garden hose out to extinguish the fire.

"God damn it Dean! You almost burned down my house!" he screamed. I knew Elmer was grumpy but had no idea he was capable of this type of fury. He looked like a madman standing there on our porch flailing his arms in exasperation, his wispy gray hair all askew and his eyes wild with rage. I was never scared of him before but I was now. He was crazy yelling at Dad that way. People who knew Dad didn't yell at him. That was plain dangerous considering his volatility. Dad was able to side-step police intervention and calm Elmer down. Dad always knew just what to say. He was a professional back-peddler and removing his ass from a sling was an artform he had managed to perfect. He was masterful.

CHAPTER 7

"Spam" is a food group…
Mom is certain of it

The aerospace industry paid a handsome salary, but no one would have known that judging from the sad state of our family's financial situation. Dad did not concern himself with managing the money responsibly, and Mom relinquished complete control of our household finances to him. Having a narcissist with an addictive personality in charge of your family's financial destiny is quite a challenge. I never experienced stability. It always felt like the bottom was going to drop out. I knew our family was in financial trouble, and it was humiliating.

Mom was allotted a small amount of money for groceries, and she made more casseroles and meatloaf than I care to remember. She really knew how to stretch her dollar and was famous for somehow making a meal out of nothing. "What are we going to have for dinner Mom? There's nothing to eat" I'd say. "There is plenty to eat in here" she'd say, as she pulled some leftovers out of the fridge. She'd mix together some corn and green beans from days past and heat them up with some butter. Then make some macaroni and cheese and throw some Spam in it. Spam, I would find, was a staple in our house and doubled as meat when we didn't have enough money to buy the real thing. Mom would zip the can open, remove that salty chunk of whatever it was, and slice it up to serve with some potatoes or whatever leftovers she found in the fridge. We ate so much Spam that to this day, I cannot stomach the sight of it. Mom even recycled the milk served at dinner. If we didn't finish it that night, it went in the fridge to use the next day on our cereal, and in a real pinch she would just add water right into the milk carton to make it stretch a little longer. Nothing went to waste.

Our cupboards often looked bare, and Mom only did the grocery shopping once every couple of weeks. I always went with Mom to the store and knew enough not to ask for anything. No nonessentials would or could be purchased, and I was keenly aware of this fact. Mom told me years later how embarrassed she was when I asked her in front of the checker if she was writing another "rubber check." I didn't know what the phrase meant; I had just heard Mom and Dad refer to the checks that had bounced.

Dad never seemed to have any shortage of his coffee ice-cream, but we had very little to pack in our lunches. I always kept the contents of my lunch in a brown paper bag, slipping the food out quickly in hopes no one would notice its hodge-podge nature or the heel of bread on my sandwich. When there was nothing to pack, I got resourceful and made sandwiches using saltines. I'd smear them with some peanut butter or jelly, depending on which one we had, and when kids commented, I acted as though it was my favorite lunch. Buying a school lunch could be equally embarrassing… thirty years later I still remember the humiliation I felt handing the lunch lady two rolls of pennies.

Our clothing situation was no better. When a neighborhood girl who lived across the street brought over a bag of clothes she had outgrown, I don't know whether I felt more grateful or embarrassed. I got four outfits at the beginning of the school year- almost enough to wear a different outfit each day of the week. I was careful to preserve them, knowing full well I would not see any new clothes until Christmas. One year, Mom and Dad didn't have the money to buy us any school clothes. Grandma and grandpa took us shopping that year.

Mom seemed to make up for all that we lacked with her resourcefulness. She scrimped and made do with very little. When things around the house needed repair, she would fix them herself or improvise. When the agitator on our washing machine remained broken for over a month, she used a baseball bat to poke and plunge away at our clothes. She always found a way to make things work…with little complaint.

Spattered in between our perpetual state of deprivation, Dad would defiantly ignore the reality of our situation and somehow finance large purchases for himself - like a motorcycle or a new car. I don't know if Dad knew we were poor. He did not live in a state of want like the rest of us. This was simply not his experience. He used the money to buy whatever he wanted, while Mom cut coupons and rolled change for groceries. I don't think he even noticed the lack of food or clothing in our household. Maybe, he just didn't care. Bottom line, Dad made sure his needs were met and did not concern himself with anything else.

When Dad was not purchasing luxury items for himself, he was gambling a good chunk of our family's earnings at the local casinos. That was why we were poor. Gambling was an interesting endeavor for Dad. Most people who compulsively gamble ultimately study the game and justify their behavior by creating some "fool-proof" strategy. Basically, a set of rules to follow they believe will result in winning. Not Dad…his gut instincts dictated his reckless style. He played Blackjack…rather poorly, I might add. It was not uncommon to find him alone at a table playing multiple hands at one time. I imagine he was alone at the table because no one wanted to play with a man who wantonly and arbitrarily "hit" and "stayed" on cards you should never "hit" or "stay" on.

When Dad began disappearing for days at a time to gamble at the local casinos, things became dire and Mom turned desperate. Most of the time, Dad's trips to the casinos were unplanned, and he just wouldn't come home from work. He'd finally call Mom long after dinner and tell her where he was. His timing was good. His telephone call usually came after Mom's anger had subsided and turned to frantic uncertainty. She would always hang up feeling grateful Dad had telephoned, believing he was on his way home as promised. She would wait and wait, but Dad wouldn't come home.

Then she'd spend half the night calling the local casinos trying to track him down.

Mom spent countless nights searching for Dad. Her glass of wine kept her company and offered some comfort. I didn't know it at the time, but Adam would often stay up late to console her. No wonder he was so damn serious…he had the weight of the world on his shoulders. Dad's gambling had indeed become compulsive, and his moral standing seemed to stoop to new depths. He routinely pilfered away his earnings. Mom responded by crying. Her loyalty remained remarkably unwavering. She would not leave him. Unfortunately, her forgiveness seemed only to fuel Dad's rotten behavior. It somehow justified the irrational. I think Dad believed Mom's clemency suggested *permission*.

Something was missing for Dad. Something he couldn't seem to identify or fulfill. I often wondered if he gambled to appease his addiction or to sabotage his marriage and alienate Mom. *Everything Dad loved got abused.* Strangely, he seemed to embrace the chaos and was recharged by the risks he took, even when they involved losing everything he loved.

And like a spoiled child, Dad continued to do all the things that eroded our family. He seemed oblivious and indifferent to the damage he caused. "See you later Am" he'd say. "Where are you going Dad?" "I'm going to get lucky" he'd reply unapologetically. Thankfully, I did not ask him to explain what "getting lucky" meant. In retrospect, I believe it suggested more than one meaning…lucky with cards and with women.

Dad thought that if he delivered the truth, it would somehow completely pardon the inexcusable. He really prided himself as being an imparter of truth. He believed we all owed him a debt of gratitude for his honesty…like he deserved a fucking medal or something. I did appreciate Dad's honesty, but it often hurt, and I was a glutton for punishment. *Do you like my picture Dad?... No. Daddy, is Santa Clause real?... No. Do you want to play? ... No.* After a while, I learned some questions were better not asked.

Dad could not see his behavior realistically. Maybe, he was completely content with the dilapidated state of our family or perhaps he was just oblivious to it. One thing I am certain of... Dad did not care how his behavior impacted the rest of us. No doubt, I felt victimized, but being a victim must not have suited me. Over the next three years something happened. I was no longer shy and needy; rather, I was sufficiently pissed off. I have tried to pinpoint a single factor that might explain my serious shift in personality, but it simply had to be self-preservation. I adapted to Mom's rigidness juxtaposed with Dad's recklessness. Sometimes I wonder whether Mom was rigid to offset Dad, or whether Dad was reckless to offset Mom. They just couldn't seem to strike a balance, and Dad's larger than life personality demanded submission and gobbled us up. Mom surrendered and adapted to Dad by drinking wine and creating and controlling a superficial order all around her. Adam, who was sensitive and introspective, adapted by stuffing down his feelings, and I adapted by becoming angry. At the time, I had no idea why I was angry, but it did seem to offer some semblance of power in a powerless situation. My anger would protect me and I wasn't going down without a fight.

CHAPTER 8

Lord of the Flies

"Hey Am, have you ever seen a match burn twice?" Dad asked. "No," I said enthralled. Dad carefully swiped the match against the striker and let the fire dance down the stick. "Well, that's one." Then he blew the match out and pressed the still glowing end against my arm. I jumped, startled by the searing pain and looked at Dad with hurt confusion. "Don't you get it Am? The match burned twice!" Dad said, as he laughed unapologetically.

When I was in the fifth grade, Dad got laid off and was out of work. Subsequently, our family's financial situation got worse than it already was…if that was possible. Dad was in the bathtub when some guy came to our door asking if an adult was home. Dad abruptly got out of the tub and stood there still dripping wet to see our car get repossessed. If recollection serves…I think he ran out with his gun to thwart the repossession.

Mom ended up getting a job working swing shift at a paper factory to make ends meet and overnight, she became virtually unavailable. We didn't see her in the morning because she was asleep before we left for school, and we didn't see her at dinner because she didn't get home till midnight. She wasn't there after school to greet us; that was now Dad's job. Dinner was also Dad's job, which usually meant if mom hadn't prepared something in advance, you were on your own. Any kind of order Mom had managed to establish over the years was immediately derailed and a "Lord of the Flies" fend for yourself ethos took hold.

There really were no rules other than the unfair ones Dad made up spontaneously and arbitrarily…like the one he made up about purchases made from the ice-cream man. One day, I used two dollars I managed to save to buy some popsicles and candy from the ice-cream man. When I returned home, Adam was strong-arming me for the goods and a squabble ensued. Dad came to mediate and decided that *"starting now"*, all purchases made from the ice-cream man would be divvied up. He and Adam then helped themselves to my goodies. Routine injustices such as this kept my embers of anger well stoked.

Guidance was given strictly on a "Do as I say, not as I do" basis. My decisions were really my own to make, and I was burdened by the enormity of that challenge. I sorted out my own problems and internalized everything. I told Dad what I planned to do, and there was absolutely no interference. He just let me make mistakes and learn by them. Occasionally, he would offer me a piece of bad advice like "Hey, why don't you play marbles on the freeway," just to see if I was able to filter his rubbish.

On top of the chaos at home, school was taking a turn for the worse. I had a terrible teacher that year. She seemed to hold a special grudge against me that I did not deserve or understand. All my teachers had liked me in the past, and in turn I worked especially hard for them. I'd simply never had a teacher dislike me, and it felt wretched. I quickly decided that if my teacher didn't like me, I certainly was not going to like her, so I mirrored that disdain right back at her, thereby earning myself some detentions after school.

To make matters worse, an older sixth grade girl was bullying me at school. I don't think her day was complete, unless she verbally chastised me. Her abuse was progressive and finally got physical during a kickball game, when she shoved me in front of everyone. I had literally had it. Things were coming to a head and my mind was made up. I knew exactly what I was going to do, and I informed Dad of my decision.

That morning, I got up and told Dad, "I'm going to get into a fight today at school." He replied, "Kick her ass!" I went to school that day ready to unleash my anger on that girl. Not only to punish her for mistreating me, but to collect a debt of injustice owed to me by the universe. I was going to enjoy her reaction of utter shock when she saw me: this inconspicuous little white girl, morph into a rabid dog. I would let her hit me first and then I would feel completely justified in annihilating her.

I had been completely empowered to right the wrongs. Yes, it would feel so good to kick that girl's ass. Sure enough, she confronted me as she always did, and we decided to meet after school in the bike racks. I showed up fully prepared to fight, but she did nothing but stand there. We stared each other down and then she walked away. She never bothered me again. I was no longer afraid.

Even though Dad provided little guidance, he was a strong ally. I could usually depend on him to take my side, even when I was wrong. He had an uncanny ability to question "ethics," and since his moral compass was askew, he could debate the topic with convincing power; even the most principled individual walked away questioning himself after disputing with Dad.

That year, Dad had empowered me to take control of a bully. Then I had the satisfaction of watching him deal with the teacher who had also bullied me the better half of the year. When I brought my report card home at the end of the year, Dad spent more time than usual looking it over. I wasn't pushed academically. Mom and Dad just told me to do the best I could. I was an above average student by choice, and despite my terrible teacher, that year was no different. I had managed to earn all "A's" with the exception of one "B."

Dad got a smirk on his face and said, "Amber, how in the world did you manage to earn nearly straight A's and be given all unsatisfactory marks in citizenship? That is an impossible contradiction." "I know Dad, it doesn't make any sense. Are you mad?" Dad chuckled and said, "Oh, I'm not mad. Go get me the phone." I grabbed the phone off the night stand. "Who are you calling, my teacher?" "I'm calling the goddamn principal. I can't wait for his explanation!"

Dad railed on the principal for the absurdity of my report card and insisted a reasonable explanation be given, but the principal simply could not provide one. He agreed that the discrepancy flew in the face of rea-son...and this pleased both me and Dad. Dad was probably secretly proud that I was able to pull off such a feat…earning both "A's" and "U's." *It was an underdog victory…I was my father's daughter.*

CHAPTER 9

The Void Strikes Again

Mom was horrified when Dad came home driving a motorcycle. "Dean, you know I hate motorcycles! Whose bike is this?" "It's mine!" "No, Why Dean?" Mom moaned. "Come on, you are going to love it. Get on the back I'll give you a ride." "I'll take a ride Dad!" I said eagerly, running my fingers across the shiny black paint. "No! You are not allowed on that motorcycle, Amber." Mom yelled. "Come on Mom!" "Absolutely not!" Mom was furious. We didn't have money for a motorcycle, and Mom knew darn well that the likelihood of Dad killing himself on that thing was high. Dad was beaming and manic and immediately began soliciting rides to the neighbors who had started to gather.

Dad took off down our street with a neighbor on the back *"Vroom!"* Mom seemed angry for a few minutes, but when I turned back to look at her as Dad ripped out of the driveway, I saw half of her mouth tilt up to form a smirk. Mom wanted Dad to be happy. When he was happy, she was happy, and Dad only seemed satisfied when he was experiencing new, intense sensations. For him, all the feelings in between were monotonous, even depressing. He simply wasn't living when things were not exciting, and Mom seemed content to have her feelings secondary to his.

Dad zipped around on the motorcycle, but Mom had little interest in the bike. She eventually took a ride or two, but it scared her. *It should have.* Mom's indifference to Dad's toy didn't seem to bother him. He rode that motorcycle around town and when his aerospace job called him to return to work after his lay-off, he drove his bike to work.

While Dad was laid off from work, he used much of his time to connect with old friends and make some new ones around town. It wasn't uncommon to see the mailman stop mid-route at our house to join Dad for a beer. I suspect Dad was picking his brain, considering whether it would be interesting or lucrative to break into the mail delivery service. Dad also made friends with the local donut shop owner and convinced him to give him all the day-old donuts. Dad would wake up early and load the old donuts into a big hefty bag. Then he would mount his motorcycle, sling the bag over his shoulder like Santa, and ride to work toting all those smashed together donuts. Needless to say, this made him quite the celebrity at work. I guess none of his coworkers cared what the donuts looked like. They gobbled them up, and when Dad had none to offer they would inquire, "Where are the donuts Dino?" Operating a motorcycle while holding a hefty bag full of old donuts must have posed its difficulties, but Dad only lost the bag once, strewing dozens of day-old donuts all over the freeway.

The motorcycle seemed to satisfy Dad's need for danger and excitement for a short time, but nothing ever seemed to permanently satiate his intense desires. There was a void that he could not ever seem to fulfill. Its pursuit made him self-destructive. It called to him, made him crazy, and its appeal threatened to pulverize him. I don't think Dad fully recognized the existence of the *void*. He didn't understand it…none of us did.

Dad finally did crash the motorcycle, just as we all knew he would. He went to a bar on his lunch break and on the way back to work he leaned too far while traveling the curve of the on- ramp and the bike tipped over. The bike skidded on its side for yards with Dad still crouched on top of it like a surfer riding a wave. Sparks flew everywhere, and as the bike slowed Dad bailed out into the ice plants and rolled over and over down an embankment until his body came to a stop. Other than a hole in the back of his jeans and road rash covering one of the cheeks of his butt, Dad was unscathed. He had cheated death once again. *I'll bet he had a smile on his face as he slid across the freeway atop that bike.*

I was in the sixth grade when I decided I was going to be in the Olympics. As far as I was concerned, the fact that I attended the "Cathy Rigby Academy" proved I was as worthy as any Olympian. In retrospect, I was delusional. Aside from being able to do some impressive back hand-springs, I was a mediocre gymnast at best.

I remember it vividly. I was perched on the lower parallel bar attempting a new trick I had learned. I lifted off the bar and swung myself forward and came crashing down on the mat. The sound of my fall echoed throughout the gym with such a thunderous clap that every head swiveled my way to assess the damage. I was utterly humiliated by the fall and popped up quickly to dust myself off. I was such a stubborn and prideful kid. I knew instantly that I had broken my hand, but I couldn't bear for anyone to see me cry, so I just acted as though nothing was wrong. When the pain became unbearable, I showed the instructor my swollen hand, and she sent me to the office for some ice. I had been sitting for a while with an ice pack on my hand when my friend's mom came to pick us up. My hand was now throbbing angrily and had started to turn a shade of purple. When I got home, I looked around for Dad, but he was nowhere to be found. I searched the house and saw the plastic patio chair next to our backyard fence and felt a sudden pang of disappointment. *"Shit, Dad is in the ditch again...who knows when he will be back,"* I thought.

Dad had begun escaping home life more and more by retreating into the Santa Ana river bed directly over our backyard fence. This behavior seemed to happen right about the time Mom got the job at the paper factory. Funny, when you are a kid, you don't think to ask pertinent questions. You just generally accept what *is*. I had no idea what Dad was doing in the ditch, what took him so long once he got there, or why he needed to arm himself with his BB gun. It didn't really dawn on me to ask Dad any questions …maybe I just didn't want to know. Mom must have known something though, because she hated it when he disappeared over the fence for hours. They fought about it. With Dad gone in the ditch and Mom at work, I had no choice but to wait. The pain in my hand throbbed with every beat of my heart. I paced the house and even got up on the chair to yell for Dad in the ditch, but he was nowhere in sight.

A couple of hours later, Dad finally emerged from the ditch. I told him what happened at the gym and showed him my swollen hand, but he didn't seem concerned. "It's broken Dad, I know it. It's killing me; I need to go to the hospital." I looked into Dad's eyes, pleading for him to take me, and noticed that something was off. He was acting differently, much giddier and distracted than usual. "Let's get you some aspirin, you'll be just fine," he told me. I followed Dad to the bathroom where he doled out several pills into his hand. He gave me two and said, "I'll take some too!" We each took our pills and I retreated to my room.

I knew Mom would have handled the situation differently, but she was working at the paper factory and wouldn't be home until midnight. I resolved that nothing could be done until the morning, and I would simply have to wait. I lay there that night barely able to sleep, frequently waking to the throbbing pain in my hand. The following day, I woke Mom and told her what happened. She took me to the doctor, who confirmed the broken bones in my hand. I left with a cast up to my elbow feeling bitter towards Dad. He had let me down… again.

Poor Mom, I think all the years of stress and anxiety coping with Dad's antics had simply taken their toll. If she wasn't born with a "Type A" personality, she had certainly developed one over the years and she was wound tighter than a banjo. Mom came from a traditional family. Her parents were just like "The Cleavers," the epitome of wholesomeness. Mom thought that she would marry the man she loved and be taken care of for the rest of her life, just like her own folks. This obviously wasn't happening, but Mom believed in the idea of marriage and she would not give up, even when it promised her own destruction. Dad continued to gamble and took a liking to prostitutes. Even when he came home with crabs, Mom was full of forgiveness. I think Mom took so much abuse that it created the challenge Dad was looking for. The challenge of finding the source of what could possibly destroy the remnants of his marriage…and he was on a mission.

Mom was the glue responsible for holding everything together at home and she was overwhelmed by this mammoth undertaking. Dad did nothing to help around the house. Mom raised us kids, did the cleaning, cooking, shopping, household maintenance, and took Adam to his baseball games. She painted the house, hung wallpaper, did the gardening, you name it. She was full of anxiety all the time and she was exhausted. I assume that's why she started drinking.

I was about eleven years old when Dad walked into the kitchen and told me and Adam, "Kids, your Mom is an alcoholic." I didn't really believe Dad. Yes, Mom drank alcohol, but an alcoholic? Dad told us that we were going to help Mom out and began pulling bottles of wine out of the pantry, eight bottles at least. He gave me and Adam two bottles each and said, "Follow me."

We followed Dad out to the backyard and he chucked a bottle of Mom's wine over the fence into the ditch. He was really pleased with himself and told us, "Okay, throw it all over." It seemed like fun, so Adam and I took turns throwing Mom's wine over the fence, pausing to hear it shatter on the other side. Mom was not pleased when she came home and learned her stash of wine had been annihilated. However, she just bought more.

Dad was really good at identifying other people's problems but couldn't see his own. I don't even think Dad knew that in large part *he* was the reason Mom drank.

CHAPTER 10

Dad was a drug addict, but he was crazy before that.

Mom and Dad argued plenty, but that morning, a gloomier tone weighed heavy in the house. Mom and Dad's fighting got so ugly that they asked me and Adam to go outside and play. It was about 8:00 am on a Saturday, and nobody was out playing. Most of the neighborhood was still sleeping. So, Adam and I sat side by side near the trash cans on the side of the house. Something was wrong. Mom and Dad never asked us to go outside while they fought. A serious concern crept over me. "Adam, do you think Mom and Dad are going to get a divorce?" I asked. "Shut up, just shut up!" he replied. Right then, I knew with certainty the answer was a resounding "Yes." A frightening calm came over me. Was I relieved? I sat a long while contemplating my treasonous feelings, then heard Mom calling for us. Adam and I went to our parent's room where my Dad was still lying in bed, and before we could sit down he growled, "Kids, me and your Mom are getting a divorce. Now get out!"

Adam and I stood there flabbergasted. I'm not sure what I loathed more, the announcement itself or its indifferent delivery. Mom was heartbroken and tried to initiate a healthy, nurturing discussion, but Dad wouldn't have it. Dad's shocking decree concluded not only the conversation, but our family as we knew it forever.

I don't know if Mom and Dad had a conversation about how insensitive Dad's divorce announcement was or whether the improved tone in the house was relief on Mom's part, but in the coming days, they put on friendly faces. They reassured us that they loved one another but simply could not live together anymore. I was in the sixth grade and Adam was a freshman in high school. Adam was taking it much harder than I was, probably because he was the one responsible for figuring things out for Mom. She didn't know what to do, and so she shut down. She left Adam in charge of finding a place for us to live, and he took the task on just as he did everything else that was asked of him.

Dad and I were sitting in the kitchen when he told Mom that he wanted me to live with him. Dad paid little attention to me. I was surprised he wanted me. It felt good, despite how awful I knew it would be living with him. I would have gone with him. I would have coped with the dysfunction, however bad, just to feel loved. But Mom quickly said, "No, Amber is coming with me." Dad didn't put up a fight; he had probably asked for Adam first anyway...*asshole!*

Mom should have hired an attorney. She was no match for Dad and his vindictiveness scared her. But, Dad convinced Mom that they had no use for lawyers because the divorce was "amicable." They could simply file the divorce paperwork themselves. It would be a snap. A "For Sale" sign was erected in our front yard on a sturdy wood post, proof of our family's failure for all to gaze at. Potential buyers traipsed in and out of the house, but nothing happened. The house did not sell. As the weeks passed, Mom and Dad were really starting to get on one another's nerves. They were still sharing the same bed, and Mom started "going out" after work, which really pissed Dad off. To make matters worse, Mom and Dad told us the divorce was our "family business," and this information was not to be shared with anyone. I was sad and lonely but too afraid to tell anyone what was happening...not even my best friend.

While we were waiting for the house to sell, other matters needed to be dealt with. Dad called me into the living room one Saturday and told me we were going to go around the house to "divide the assets." I was responsible for remembering "who got what." I didn't have a piece of paper or a pen to write things down; I just committed the information to memory. We didn't have a whole lot, so it wasn't difficult. Mom and Dad quarreled about one item, a round crystal vase. It was a wedding gift from my Mom's uncle, but Dad was relentless, and the arguing persisted. Finally, Mom won. I think

Dad feigned his desire for the vase just to make Mom feel grateful for his *generosity* when he surrendered the item to her.

As time passed waiting for the house to sell, Mom and Dad forgot "who got what" and would yell, "Amber get in here, whose is this!" I somehow remembered and would stop the arguing by announcing, "That's Mom's" or "That's Dad's." Adam busied himself with more pressing matters. He needed to figure out where we were going to live. He looked through newspapers to find an apartment in the area so we could stay in Cerritos and attend the same schools. But after he crunched the numbers factoring in Mom's low pay at the paper factory and the $300.00 Dad agreed to pay for child support, he quickly realized we were screwed. We couldn't even afford an apartment.

There was no way Mom could afford to house, clothe, and feed us. Mom contested the $300.00 and asked for more support, but Dad told her if she wanted to fight about the amount, he would give her nothing instead. Mom accepted his ultimatum and felt she had no options. Adam sat down with Mom and laid out the gloomy forecast of our future, and it was decided that the only thing to do was to ask Grandma and Grandpa, Mom's folks, if we could come live with them.

My last day at Cerritos Elementary School fell right before Christmas break. I cried and said goodbye to my friends, but they just couldn't understand what happened or why I had to leave so suddenly. They were confused and so was I. I hadn't told anyone what was happening. My teacher, Mr. Duckworth, seemed saddest of all. I was close to him and even did activities outside of school with him and other students. He made me feel special, a feeling I was not used to and missed at home.

Mr. Duckworth got tears in his eyes and asked, "Why didn't you tell me this was going on?" I don't know why I held this secret for months. I guess

I was used to holding secrets. Mr. Duckworth was the one person who believed in me fully and had gone to great lengths to show me how special I was, a surrogate father of sorts...why hadn't I told him? I had disappointed him. I hadn't trusted him. I had been too scared. I gave him a big hug and left crying, angry with myself. *I wish I had told him.*

Mom, Adam, and I arrived at Grandma and Grandpa's house on a Saturday morning. Grandma and Grandpa were full of love and they welcomed us right into their home. I loved them but living with them was a little humiliating. Our family had failed, and Mom and us kids could not make it on our own. I think everyone thought that the situation was "temporary," but it wasn't.

Mom and I shared a room with a queen-sized bed, and Adam got his own room. We enjoyed Christmas break and when it was over, Mom enrolled me in a nearby school, so I could finish out the sixth grade. I had beautiful long blond hair that hung all the way to my lower back, and within a month of moving in with Grandma and Grandpa I cut it all off. My hair was so short, I looked like a boy. I instantly regretted the decision and felt ugly. After lopping off my hair, I pierced my own ears--several holes in each lobe. I pushed the needle through the tissue of my earlobes slowly and got a strange satisfaction from the popping noises my flesh made as the needle breached the other side. For some inexplicable reason, that pain felt really good.

Within a year of Mom and Dad's divorce, Dad was engaged. Dad told me that he asked the woman to marry him after she put two "Ben Wa Balls" in her vagina and couldn't get them out. Dad said she jumped up and down and gravity wouldn't even budge those heavy things. Apparently, a tight pussy went a long way in Dad's book; it superseded a family anyway. I didn't know how to feel about the situation until I met the woman…what a bitch. She was from North or South Carolina, one of the two, and worked with Dad in the aerospace facility. She was a petite thing and was way too young for Dad. She had no intention of forming a relationship with me or Adam, but it didn't matter. Within weeks, the marriage was annulled.

Dad seemed tortured by the woman, and deservedly so. He said that her hypoglycemia made her unbearable, but her dogs seemed to seal the deal on the dissolution of their marriage. Dad seemed jealous of the animals and couldn't stand the fact that she treated her dogs better than him. Dad said, "The only marriage that counts, is the first anyway." Mom was hurt by Dad's choice to remarry so soon. It cheapened their marriage.

We had only been living with Grandma and Grandpa a short time before things started getting really interesting. Mom began acting like a teenager and was eager to go out on the town to dance and celebrate her "newly single" status. She dated a string of losers, finally settling for the youngest one, and began dating him exclusively. This was nothing compared to Dad's mid-life crisis. After he divorced his second wife, he paired up with an equally depraved roommate who he worked with in aerospace.

I knew things were bad when I arrived at Dad's house and saw women's panties covering the entire living room wall. Panties of every size and color-- big ones, little ones, pink ones, used ones, ripped ones. There must have been sixty pairs! Dad stood there beaming with pride at his fantastic panty collection, noting that most of them had indeed been worn and not washed before being hung. *Jesus, where were Child Protective Services when you needed them?*

Oddly, at the time, the colorful panty art wall did not seem *that* strange. Clearly, I was already hardened to serious dysfunction. Dad suggested I hand over my underwear to add to the glorious shrine, but I opted not to relinquish it. In addition to the panty wall, Dad had some paraphernalia around the house he felt needed introduction. He took great joy in explaining the various uses for his whips, Ben Wa Balls, and other sadomasochistic toys. Dad and his new roommate reveled in the ridiculous brothel-like scene they had created, and Dad thought it totally appropriate to freely discuss his sexual escapades with me.

Dad and his roommate had mutual interests and with no pesky family around, Dad's behavior quickly spiraled out of control. He overdosed on an eight ball of cocaine that year. Apparently, he snorted enough coke to kill a horse, spoke to Jesus, then went out to get the mail completely naked. Had the mailman not found him, and sought help, he probably would have died.

I remember Mom taking me to the drug treatment hospital to see Dad. He lay there in the bed skinny, wild eyed, and shaking. Dad's legs wouldn't stop moving. They bounced around as he reassured me and Mom that he was "just fine." I looked over at the guy in the bed next to Dad. His nose appeared eaten away, almost completely gone. I started to cry and wondered if that was how Dad would end up.

Still good humored, Dad lit up a cigarette and laughed his naughty laugh before the nurse came in to scold him. "Sir, you can't smoke in here!" "They taste so much better when they aren't allowed," Dad snickered. I thought Dad was going to die in short order and when I went home, I sat down and wrote his Eulogy, the first of many ....

CHAPTER 11

"I'll love your father till the day I die."

-Mom

Dad wasn't always a drug addict. He was introduced to cocaine when he started working in aerospace in the 1980's. Apparently, using cocaine was pretty commonplace in the industry, and it was not unusual for his coworkers to lay out a line of coke on their tool box and snort it right there at work. Don't ask me how management was not aware of this fact, because that, I will never know. Anything deemed *against the rules* appealed to Dad, and drugs were no exception, so I doubt he had any reservation accepting the offer to try cocaine that first time. Dad's drug addiction took hold of him when I was in the sixth grade, just prior to Mom and Dad's divorce. He was using cocaine regularly, and he had become quite flagrant about his habit. He snorted his cocaine off a framed mirrored picture. It had a picture of a woman drinking a soda and said "Enjoy Coke." This could always be found lying around the house with a razor blade and a straw sitting on top of it.

Mom disagreed with Dad's choices and chastised him, but Dad was a con man and had a way of justifying every lousy thing he did. He was so convincing that he managed to persuade Mom to try cocaine too. Luckily, she didn't have an appetite for the substance and after trying it once, she never used it again. But Dad continued to use drugs and Mom put up with him. She wouldn't leave him; she was loyal to a fault.

Dad's drug use was not the reason behind Mom and Dad's divorce. That morning they were fighting and deciding our family's destiny, Mom told Dad that she forgave him. She didn't want to get a divorce. She was willing to go the long haul and probably would have done so had it not been for Dad who said, "I just can't forgive myself, I want out." *What a lousy cop out.* Mom finally agreed to the divorce, not because she was tired of Dad's bullshit but because she didn't want to be with someone who didn't want to be with her. Dad wasn't concerned about his family, but his selfishness produced an unintended "selfless act"… he had released us.

Life with Grandma and Grandpa was fortuitous…in retrospect, they saved me and Adam. They took over parental roles when Mom and Dad disappeared, and for the first time ever I stopped fearing the "bottom dropping out."

Grandpa helped me with my homework after school, and in the evenings, he would play his soothing trumpet to a sound track… "*Mr. Sandman, bring me a dream.*" Grandma always had popsicles and made meals according to the clock. Lunch was at noon and dinner was at 5 pm. The consistency felt nice. Grandma would always say, "Hugs are free honey," and then she would hug me, my friends, or anyone else close enough for her to grab and squeeze. Ironically, Grandma was an Alcoholics Anonymous sponsor. I found it hard to imagine her as an alcoholic because she had been sober for so long. I only remember her getting drunk once. I was probably about five years old.

Grandma and Grandpa got into an argument and Grandma wanted to leave, but Grandpa took her car keys. Grandma said, "Come on Amber," and she held my hand as we walked out of the cul-de-sac and turned onto the busy street. "Where are we going Grandma?" "We are going to use the phone over here" she said. We walked a couple of blocks until we reached the pay phone, and Grandma called Mom. I was scared. Something bad was happening, and I wanted to go home. I got on the phone and began to cry. "Mommy, I want to come home!" Mom just hollered and told me I wasn't coming home and that I needed to walk back to the house with Grandma. I was frantic, but Grandma hung up the phone, remained calm, and said, "Come on." We walked back to the house as Grandma held her thumb out trying to hitch a ride. "Grandma don't hitchhike!" I yelled, "We could be taken by a stranger." "Don't worry," she said reassuringly, "I used to do this all of the time in Hawaii." Thankfully, no one pulled over to give us a lift that day, and shortly after this incident Grandma stopped drinking.

Grandma and Grandpa loved us and despite things being turned upside down, they managed to create a stable environment. Mom spent most of her time at her boyfriend's house. I was mad at her for abandoning me and Adam, but grateful knowing Grandma and Grandpa were our surrogates. They were far better equipped to act as our parents at that point. Besides, I felt sorry for Mom because she had been held captive for so long. She was finally free. I made friends at my new school and managed to stay out of trouble. Dad's presence was sparse. He was free and his interests did not include me. I, too, was free.

PART II

CHAPTER 12

Sometimes the Universe has no mercy

C huck died of a massive heart attack when I was thirteen years old. My best friend's daddy, the father I longed for, and Dad's best friend was unfathomably snatched away. Some memories are burned into our brains never to be forgotten; this one is too heartbreaking to write about. I often wonder if Chuck could have saved Dad from himself.

Sometimes the universe has no mercy.

When I was a freshman in high school, Adam was a senior. I hadn't been at the same school with Adam since elementary school, and although I rarely saw him on campus, it gave me comfort knowing he was there. Adam managed a 4.2 grade point average with his advanced placement classes, and he had his choice of colleges. He was eager to graduate and leave home. I didn't want him to go. Mom hadn't gone to college and knew nothing about getting into one, but Adam didn't seem to need her help anyway. He could have gone anywhere with his grades, but he always seemed to consider the practical side of things. There was only so much money, and it appeared that Mom was his sole financial backer.

Adam navigated the various admission processes, submitted his essays, and was accepted to San Diego State University, his school of choice. After high school graduation, Adam immediately prepared to leave home and began acquiring dorm essentials. He was excited and periodically he would break into song, "SDSU Fight, Fight, Fight!" All his hard work had finally paid off. Not to say that it was hard for *him*...he had seemingly mastered the art of earning straight A's while attending school as little as possible. His resourceful "time management" certainly must have made Dad proud. After all, how many honor students can maintain their grade point averages while regularly skipping class.

Mom trusted Adam. He had never given her reason not to. So, she allowed him to forge her name on the parent signature card two years earlier, enabling him to miss class and write his own "parental note" to legitimately excuse his absences. Adam's teachers must have felt the same way Mom did because they never questioned any of his absences. Adam was able to turn in all of his assignments and ace his tests, despite missing classes or the occasional school day.

Right at the end of Adam's senior year, he finally got busted for writing his own notes. The cranky school receptionist got suspicious and went all the way back to Adam's freshman year's parent signature card to cross reference the signatures. The signatures didn't match, despite Adam's skilled forgery, and the jig was up. Adam was given his first school disciplinary action-- Saturday school.

Attending school on a Saturday was a cruel and unusual form of punishment. Not only were you required to get up early to be there by 8:00 am, but you weren't allowed to talk and had to do school work for four hours. If you did not comply with the rules, you risked coming back the following Saturday. I had my share of Saturday school, but Adam was never in trouble. I felt bad for him.

Mom did not stand idly by. She went straight to the Dean of Discipline and demanded that he rescind the punishment. She told him she had allowed Adam to sign the parent signature card because he was a trustworthy "straight A" student. As far as she was concerned, if Adam kept his grades up, she didn't care how many days he missed. Mom could be pushy with teachers and school administrators. She believed they had no business meddling in areas she considered "parental territory." They were there to teach academics and no more. Everything else was her job and they needed to butt out. Mom had implicitly given Adam permission to sign those cards, and certainly the school's refusal to accept this fact infringed on her "parental territory." Mom put up a good argument and challenged the principal's ruling, but finally relented. Probably because deep down, she knew that she had violated the rules by allowing Adam to sign the cards in the first place- and Mom was BIG on following rules. She chose not to forge this particular battle, but had waged and won many before. She was very protective and could quickly turn into "Mama Bear," ripping someone to pieces if they threatened me or Adam.

Adam's third grade bully learned that lesson the hard way. The kid routinely stepped on the back of Adam's shoes as he walked home from school and told him "You've got flat tires!" He'd taunt Adam the entire walk home, pushing him around and stepping on his feet. Adam, pacifist that he was, would do nothing but come home in tears. One day, Mom saw Adam getting stepped on and pushed around as he walked home. She stopped our green Pinto so abruptly I thought I might be hurled through the front window of the car… kids just didn't wear seatbelts back then.

I'll never forget what happened next; it was permanently burned into my five-year-old brain. Mom cornered the kid up against the wall and proceeded to scream directly in his face, about two inches from his face to be more accurate. I know the gist of her tirade to the boy was that he was NEVER to touch Adam again. But it wasn't her words that were so intimidating; it was the tone and pitch of her screaming. I had never heard that sound come out of Mom. It was loud, shrill, and hysterical. Her voice carried so far that people on the opposite side of the street, yards away stopped to gawk. I was terrified and wasn't even the target of Mom's fury. I can only imagine how that bully felt. He never messed with Adam again.

I sometimes wonder how someone like Mom, a woman so fiercely protective, could have been so oblivious to the threat that lived right under our roof for so many years.

When I was young, maybe five or six years old, I used to ask Adam if I could work for him when I grew up. I imagined myself cleaning his house, doing his laundry, or taking care of his kids. Adam was going to make something of himself. He was destined for greatness…menial work seemed more fitting for me. Adam told me he would give me a job someday, and this gave me great peace, knowing he wouldn't let the world swallow me up. Years later, as he prepared himself for college, a part of me still believed Adam's success would keep me safe too.

Days before Adam went away to college, he stood over the bathroom sink, and I watched a string of blood pour from his nose, a snotty viscous type of blood that stretched all the way from his nose to the sink basin. Adam seemed amused, and he laughed as he pretended to pull the bloody goop from his nose like a circus clown. I was concerned and said "Oh my god Adam, what's wrong with you? This is the third bloody nose in a month...you need to see a doctor!" Adam didn't seem concerned at all. "Na, I'm fine Am, close the door behind you." I left the bathroom but couldn't dismiss my looming concern. Adam spent a lot of time at Dad's house and it was pretty obvious why Dad got so many bloody noses.

CHAPTER 13

Dad gave me flowers once

Dad gave me flowers once. Four dozen pink carnations. It was my fourteenth birthday and probably the first time I had ever felt cherished by Dad.

I saw Dad infrequently while living at Grandma and Grandpa's house. Most divorced parents set up a custody or visitation schedule but we didn't seem to need one…probably because Dad wasn't big on visiting. He just called and dropped in spontaneously when it suited him.

"I got a new toy Am!" Dad said with familiar zeal. "Let me guess… does it have tires?" "Oh, ya! It's white and goes really fast." "What kind of car Dad?" I said, unable to contain my excitement any longer. "Well, how about I drive over later and show you?" "Sounds good, what time?" "Well, it's going to be late because I've got something I've got to take care of. Will you still be up at 10:00 pm?" "For sure! I'm dying to know what you got!" "Okay, I'll see you then."

Dad pulled up right on time in a new white Corvette.

"Oh my God Dad, it's awesome!"

"She's a beauty huh? I was driving by the Chevy dealership and just couldn't resist."

"Well, I can see why. I bet she goes really fast."

"I opened her up and was doing 100 on the freeway. She was purring like a kitten. Come on, I'll take you for a ride."

I jumped in on the passenger side and sunk into the leather bucket seat. I sat so low, I thought I would not be able to see over the sprawling dashboard. Dad hopped in and flipped a U-turn in one easy maneuver of the steering wheel. The wheels squealed, and the back end of the car swayed from side to side when we tore out onto the busy street.

"Ya buddy!" Dad yelled with the familiar twinkle in his eye. We hauled around town and made it home in one piece. We were sitting in the car talking when suddenly, the vehicle's alarm sounded. I plugged my ears at the hideous noise. "Turn it off Dad!" "I'm trying." He fumbled with the keys and the dash, unable to stop the screaming alarm. A neighbor finally yelled, "Shut the fuck up" from their window, and Dad decided to drive off with the alarm still sounding. In retrospect, that car probably knew its fate…and bellowed in protest. Like all cars Dad owned, this car would be no exception; it too would meet its demise and be reduced to a crumpled heap.

When I was fifteen and a half, Dad said, "Am, it's time for you to learn how to drive." Mom hadn't suggested learning yet, and I was eager to get behind the wheel. At the time, Dad drove a sporty gray mini truck with colorful graphics on each side…the Corvette had long since been demolished. Dad's truck was a stick shift, which was intimidating, but I thought it would be pretty cool to know how to drive a car with a manual transmission. We started out in the high school parking lot after it had cleared out, and Dad gave some simple instructions. "Let the clutch out while you step on the gas," he said. "What do you mean?" Which one is the clutch? I asked. "It's the pedal on the left." I released the clutch, stepped on the gas a little, and the truck lurched forward over and over. My feet bounced around the pedals from the jolting, which just made things worse. I laughed so hard I thought I would pee my pants. Dad yelled, "Push the clutch in, brake!" I didn't know which pedal did what and the car lunged forward jostling our bodies about the cab. The lesson didn't last long before Dad called it quits, but he wasn't ready to give up. He said, "We just need a bigger parking lot."

The following week, Dad took me to a giant vacant parking lot, and we tried again. He gave me a little more instruction before we began, and this time I did much better. As soon as I got used to the clutch and figured out when to shift, Dad set up an obstacle course and said, "Okay, you are going to do five up and five back as fast as you can. Ready, set, go!" I took off like a bat out of hell as Dad periodically yelled "Shift!" I did the obstacle course over and over. I gained speeds to shift into fifth gear, and then down shifted all the way to a stop. I ground those gears and forced that stick in when it didn't want to go, all while Dad sat wild-eyed beside me.

In the span of an hour, Dad had me speeding around an obstacle course like a race car driver. He rounded out the lesson by teaching me how to "peel out" and "do donuts." I squealed around the parking lot and went around and round doing donuts while Dad sat "shotgun," beaming with pride. "Okay, Am, I will pick you up next week. You are ready for Big Bear!" He announced.

The following week, Dad picked me up and we headed up to the Big Bear mountains. I had no idea how dangerous the prospect was; it sounded like a fun adventure to me. As we traversed the mountain, I realized there was only one lane going in either direction with virtually no turn outs. I needed to be careful rounding the corners and the corners kept coming. To my right, was the cliff—literally the edge of the mountain. As we got higher and higher, I didn't dare look down. I just clenched the wheel tight and tried to remain focused.

When Dad saw that I was intent on concentrating he said, "You know, there are going to be distractions in life, especially when you are on the road." He lit up a cigarette and handed it to me." Dad I can't hold that!" I yelled. "Your friends are going to be in the car and you need to be pre-pared for this type of shit!" He said. I balanced the cigarette between my fingers while I managed to shift gears. Dad laughed and lit up another cig-arette for himself. Then he reached behind the seat and snapped a bungee cord which was stretched the length of the cab. "BANG!" I jumped in the seat, still managing to hold on to the cigarette. "Dad, stop it!" I yelled. He laughed with gusto as I struggled to regain composure. He snapped that cord every time I looked like I had become relaxed, and when the cigarette burned itself out he lit up another and handed it to me.

We made it up the mountain in one piece, but as we were descending, I rounded a corner too fast and nearly ran someone off the cliff. I will never forget the look in her wide eyes, complete fear. Dad screamed and grabbed onto the handle above his door. I squealed around the corner and the woman on the other side managed to veer to the right without careening to her death below. My hands were wet with sweat and my heart raced. There was a brief silence, and then Dad calmly said, "Okay, pull over so I can clean out my shorts." We sat for a while and laughed that I had managed to "scare the shit" out of Dad. When our hearts stopped racing, I pulled back onto the road with my legs still shaking slightly. After I had been driving for a short time and had somehow regained some confidence, Dad reached behind the seat and pulled the bungee cord again.

I was absolutely liberated when I turned sixteen and got a set of wheels. Mom had a budget of one thousand dollars and I settled for a fifteen-year-old white Datsun that had seen much better days. The paint had long since lost its shine, and the interior smelled its age. I think it might possibly have been the ugliest vehicle on the planet, but I didn't care. I was mobile and largely unsupervised. Mom had abandoned her duty to me when I was in the 6th grade shortly after the divorce when she began dating someone half her age. She stayed at his house most of the time, and Grandma and Grandpa mainly supervised my activities. As it turned out, this was pretty convenient. Ever loving and trusting of their only granddaughter, they believed all my lies and I ran amuck.

On the weekends, I told Grandma I was spending the night at a friend's house, but instead I would run the streets. Usually there was a party to go to, but when there wasn't, Dad's house was always an alternative. I knew I could show up there with a slew of friends and we wouldn't have to worry about who was buying our alcohol or cigarettes or anything else my friends wanted to partake of. Dad would supply it all.

Summer days at Dad's house were memorable. He lived in an apartment complex with a giant resort style pool. My girlfriends and I would show up in our bikinis and Dad would go nuts. Dad thought we were all beautiful. He called us "mileage" and believed that our poolside presence proved only to attract "legal tail." Dad would whip up a blender full of margaritas, and we would all traipse out to the pool. To demonstrate how very desirable he was, Dad would playfully flirt with all of us as onlookers sat gawking. His sick plan always seemed to work, and soon enough other women would gravitate to our area to investigate the commotion and try to get a little attention for themselves.

Although the good times rolled at Dad's house, bringing friends there was a dangerous prospect. His mood and behavior were unpredictable, and he had absolutely no impulse control. One time he threw a dart at my friend, which stuck right into her arm. Truly, anything could happen and probably would. Only the most trusted friends were suitable for Dad's house, at the risk of serious humiliation. All my friends were ill-equipped for the sexual harassment and illegal activity they encountered, but they responded by laughing. Sometimes, I think Dad really believed they were amused.

During my visits Dad often told me, "Amber, you are either going to be a drug addict or an alcoholic." Dad's prediction scared me. Was he right? Were these two horrible options my genetic destiny? I never wanted to be like him. I was determined to prove him wrong and vowed I would never use cocaine. Adam told me years later that Dad told him the same thing. Dad's irreverent statements didn't surprise me. What blew me away was his desire to be correct, for his predictions to become a reality. Instead of steering us away from the dangers he foresaw, he created every opportunity for us to fail. He purposely laid landmines of danger in our path. I suppose he wanted us to learn by experience too.

Dad offered me drugs on a regular basis. He justified his actions and said doing drugs with him would be safer than doing them with friends. I defiantly rejected Dad's plan for me and made my feelings about cocaine use clear. Adam evidently had not. I was sixteen years old when I saw Dad carefully lay out lines of white powder before Adam. I was furious with Dad. Adam was the first-born pleaser, with an agreeable spirit. He was the vulnerable one and Dad had managed to corrupt him. *God damn him to hell!*

I lashed out at Dad but was no match for him. He told me I was a hypocrite and said I had some gall repudiating cocaine use while I drank alcohol. I left crying that day feeling angry and confused. This was the first time I had ever stood up to Dad and told him off, and it was scary. Dad was comparing apples and oranges, but somehow managed to refute reason and make me question myself. He was genius at creating illusions that distracted from the truth. I wondered if he truly believed his own lies.

CHAPTER 14

Do something...even if it's wrong

Some fathers call their daughters "Sweetie," "Sugar Booger," or "Poo Bear." Dad's term of endearment for me was "Little Bitch" or "Slut Puppy." I didn't mind; it felt endearing to me.

My relationship with Dad was perpetually peppered with periods of retreat. Dad's behavior frustrated me, and I would often create some distance in the interest of self-preservation. But I could never stay mad for long. Dad seemed to accept me completely no matter what I did or said to him. I felt an obligation to him. I somehow still loved him.

Visits at Dad's house were volatile. He could always be found sitting at his kitchen table with a pile of cocaine and his 9-millimeter gun. He usually looked deep in thought, scrawling plans on a notepad like some mad scientist. He was always in conflict with someone or something, usually a government agency that had wronged him in some fashion. Whether he was fighting a ticket or being audited by the IRS, Dad delighted in the opportunity for outright war and would become absolutely consumed by the preparation process. He thought outside of the box and when he knew he couldn't win an argument he resorted to cheating or fighting dirty. Once, he even bribed some IRS guy with a leather briefcase. The guy took the bribe and was later fired. Dad got audited ten years in a row after that, but that didn't stop him from cheating on his taxes.

Nothing Dad did seemed to surprise or offend me. He had somehow trained me to consent to and affirm all his choices; basically, he had persuaded me to believe that I should completely accept his behavior. After all, how could I begrudge his honesty? He wasn't trying to hide anything, and he expected unconditional love and acceptance. I was a child and he was my Dad. What choice did I have but to give it to him?

"You know, they cut cocaine with all types of shit—baby laxatives, aspirin, rat poison. They mix it with that crap to help their profit margin. I like to test the purity of what I'm getting." "How do you do that Dad?" "I just take a small amount of coke and drop it in some vinegar. See how it separates? That's the stuff they cut it with" he said, pointing at the cup. "Hmm,"

I said lighting up a cigarette, totally disinterested. "Do you want to play chess?" "Ya buddy! Thought you'd never ask!" He said excitedly.

I carefully arranged the pieces on the board. Dad taught me how to play chess a year earlier, and I had been trying to win a game ever since. He would never throw a game and lose purposely to make me feel capable. He won every game we played unapologetically, and although I was often frustrated I appreciated his honesty.

I slowly moved my queen toward his knight. "Are you sure you want to do that?" Dad asked. I quickly moved the piece back and studied Dad's face, hoping he'd give away a secret. But he never gave away the answers, in chess or in life. I sat contemplating for a while and Dad hollered one of his favorite mantras, "Do something…even if it's wrong!" I moved my pawn forward one space, avoiding any real risk, and looked at Dad's face again. He smirked at my careful move, surely mocking my cowardice. While Dad waited his turn, he'd lean his head forward to snort a line of cocaine laid out on the glass table. I watched the white dust disappear as the straw made its way down the line. Dad always called cocaine his "Juice," like it was some special essence that supplied him with power. When Dad wasn't snorting his cocaine, he was rubbing it all over his gums, or putting it in his cigarette to smoke. *I hated that acrid smell.* Dad just couldn't seem to get his fill of "Juice."

"I think I'm going to get called back to work. I guess I'll go-- I've had a pretty good vacation." "That will be good Dad," I said. Dad was always getting laid off in the aerospace industry. He seemed to welcome each pink slip, but his unemployment scared the shit out of me. "Well, I'm still moving forward with my business plans. Dean's Automotive is going to buy, sell, and insure cars. I've got the business cards right here…." "That's great Dad…." Dad had been trying to duplicate a successful business like "Dino's

Printing" since he closed its doors. He was a trailblazer, a pioneer, and he had grown tired of the aerospace industry. It was no longer a challenge. Every year Dad seemed to have a new business card. He tried his hand at mobile auto detailing, automotive sales, business forms, even a hot dog cart. But nothing seemed to fill the void, and his focus was so wide and grandiose that his plans never seemed to materialize.

When Dad wasn't busy beating me at chess, he was fiddling with his gun. He'd disassemble the thing, put it back together, and then repeat the process, like he was some military boot training for war. One day he said, "You need to know how to use a gun Am. There is nothing to be afraid of. Okay, I want you to load this cartridge full of bullets first. Then I want you to practice putting the cartridge in the gun. Pull this back to chamber a bullet."

I wasn't scared of the gun. I picked that heavy thing up, ejected the cartridge the way Dad had shown me, and began taking all the bullets out. "Always make sure you check to see if a bullet is left in the chamber after you release the cartridge. Here, pull this back and give her a good look-see." Dad handed back the gun and I pulled the heavy slide back toward me to peer in. "Yep, a bullet's in there!" I announced excitedly. "Well, dump it on out of there! You don't want to go shootin' yourself!" Dad said. I'm fairly certain he left a bullet in the chamber on purpose, for the lesson's sake. After I took the bullets out of the cartridge, I put them all back in, shoved the cartridge back into the bottom of the gun and cocked it, chambering a bullet.

"Very good, now make the weapon safe" Dad said. I ejected the cartridge, pulled back the slide and dumped the bullet out of the chamber. "Ya buddy! Go ahead and pull the trigger." I pulled it without hesitation...

Click. "You got this thing down. Practice a few more times, and then we are going to go shooting!"

We went to a shooting range at a place by Dad's house in Long Beach. Dad brought his gun, but he wanted me to shoot the big ones, so he rented one too. "Wait till you shoot this baby, it will knock you on your ass!" Dad handed me the .45 caliber revolver, and I took aim. When I pulled the trigger, it kicked so hard it jutted backwards and hit me in the head. Dad laughed wildly and warned, "Lock your elbows… that thing is a cannon!" Dad and I fired away until we went through two boxes of ammunition. I felt powerful and fearless.

Like all dangerous things Dad touched, the gun would give him a learning opportunity that would go unheeded. Later that year, he blew a hole in his living room floor. He thought he had rendered the gun safe but clearly this was not the case. It was just a matter of time…Dad's hasty recklessness combined with his drug use, was a lethal combination.

CHAPTER 15

"Amber, I'd love you even if you were a hooker with crabs."

-Dad

In high school, I seemed to seek out relationships equally crappy to that of my parents. Any boy with a peaceful, gracious soul was not appealing or interesting, and I discarded him and any chance of being treated with any loving kindness. Somehow, I sifted through a number of really sweet high school boys who brought me flowers and wrote me poems and settled for Max, who had just been released from a year's stint at a "bad boy" school in Utah. I ran into him at a high school party and remembered him from junior high. I always thought he was cute and we got to talking. He told me all about "rehab" and his terrible drug problem. He was perfectly hopeless and instantly provided me with a purpose. I would fix him.

Our relationship was immature and destructive, but this was evident to everyone but me. Max cheated on me, I cheated on him. We fought incessantly, and I slapped him like he was a child. He broke up with me every other week, I suspect because he wanted to feel the pain and excitement of our relationship over and over again. Every time he broke up with me, I vowed I would never return, only to go right back. The intensity was addictive and I could see no future without him.

I don't know whether I was more madly in love with him or the purpose he supplied me with. For three and a half years, I diligently worked to keep him clean and make him "better." No matter how badly he treated me, I was not going to quit. I would not have given up, probably ever, had he not *given me up* first. Max had come a long way and was living a clean life, *thanks to me.* I had spent the better part of my high school years seeing that he stayed away from drugs, and as we entered college things seemed better between us. We loved one another, and our relationship had grown more mature, but the past haunted us. We had heaped so much hurt on one another there was no way we could make it work any longer.

One night, Max told me he planned to move out of state to attend a different community college. Obviously, I thought I was included in the plan and asked him when we were leaving. I was prepared to follow him anywhere. When he told me that he needed to "do it alone," I was devastated. *Alone! The only reason he was even alive was because of me. I saved him. I fixed him, now he was just going to leave?*

My first response, despite my anger, was to tell him that I would wait for him to return, no matter how long it took. But when I thought how utterly preposterous it was that he needed to go away to attend *community college*, the anger quickly returned. He hadn't even graduated high school and was barely disciplined enough to attend the community college down the street. Who the hell goes out of state to attend community college anyway? Clearly, this was just another instance when he wanted to elicit a reaction from me so that I could reassure him how impossible life was without him.

I didn't take him seriously until I went to his house one night and learned that his plans were quite shockingly in full swing. He had an address in Utah and a roommate. This was really going to happen. That night, Max's dad stood there pleased with himself and offered me an uncustomary greeting to rub in what he had obviously facilitated. *What an asshole!* Clearly, he did not know or appreciate the fact that I had single handedly *saved* his fucking son! I promptly grabbed my keys off the counter and headed for the door. Max asked, "Where are you going?" I replied, "Just to my car to get something." Without so much as a goodbye, I got in my car and drove away feeling numb.

I wouldn't let anyone hurt me. I was too strong and too proud and would end things just like that, on my terms. Maybe Max needed more closure than I did, or maybe he knew my purpose had already been fulfilled. He found me later that night to talk. I told him, "All I need you to do is tell me you don't see me in your future." He said, "Amber, I *never* want you to be my wife." I think my mouth may have been hanging open, aghast by his apathy, but I turned on my heel, got into my car, and he walked out of my life forever.

I had picked someone just like Dad, tirelessly *fixed him*, only to be abandoned again. What purpose did I serve now? I was positively heartbroken. I sat in my car and sobbed with my head and arms slung over the steering wheel. I wept like someone had died, *something had died.* When I finally stopped crying, I vowed it would be the last time I shed a single tear over Max. With my anger firmly restored, I was released from my sadness. Anger felt familiar, gratifying.

I was nineteen years old and attending college at the time. Max had picked a hell of a time to abandon me. Grandma and Grandpa were retiring, and they planned to move to a smaller house to live out their golden years. They were selling the house, and everyone needed to move. I was screwed. Living with Grandma and Grandpa at their new house was out of the question, and the prospect of being roommates with Mom made me cringe. I was resourceful, but complete independence seemed impossible. I was working 30 hours a week, carrying a full load at school and only making a few hundred dollars a month. What was I going to do? Doing nothing seemed easiest. I was in complete denial of my situation. I just wanted it to go away, but it simply wouldn't.

Mom said, "I need to know if you want to live together, because I will buy a two-bedroom instead of a one-bedroom condominium. You will need to contribute if I buy the bigger place." *How was I going to tell Mom that I would rather be homeless than live with her?* A sense of despair weighed heavily on my soul. I was alone. No Max, no Adam, no Grandma and Grandpa…so I turned to the unthinkable…Dad.

I called Dad on the phone and told him how desperate and hopeless my situation was. I didn't know how he would respond to my pleas for advice and help. He usually only took on burdens that benefited him. Once I told Dad that I was concerned about living with Mom without us killing one another, he happily obliged to help and said, "Amber, go rent a room. Hell, go rent a house and pick your own roommates, I've got your back." I reiterated my financial situation and told Dad it would be impossible for me without his help. Dad said, "Don't worry Am, I've got your back, now go find a place to live." Two days later I received a letter in the mail from Dad.

Hey A,

Not to worry! Maintain your plans in school this is important! There are many alternatives open to you with respect to your grandparents move this coming September. Get an approximate date from them regarding their plans to move into their new home. With this target date, I will help you make your decisions come true, whatever alternative you choose.

All you must do is decide which way would be best for you. It will be fun, no matter which way you go and I won't let you fail. This will be a no-lose situation darling, so keep smiling. This has to take place sooner or later and you get to make the decision. Things just don't get better than that! Parents have such a hard time cutting loose their kids! I just don't understand their logic sometimes. It's really simple: Teach em well, give them the truth, then cut em loose. 1,2,3. Oh ya, #4, give em some money to operate with until they feel comfortable enough to send out bills to get their own package going. You have any problem with that? I didn't think so. You know all there is to know. Keep it simple. Have some fun and help others along the way. I love ya babe. Keep smiling.

Again, look forward to these changes that are about to come. This is a good step and I'm eager to be by your side to make this transition as comfortable as possible.

Your no sweat- Dad loves you.

I was floored. I don't know what surprised me more, his willingness to help or my willingness to depend on him…the most unreliable man on Earth. I had no options, so I thanked Dad and set out to find a place to live.

As it turned out, finding a place was not as easy as I thought. Renting a room seemed the best option. I was too scared to find my own place and choose my own roommates as Dad had suggested. I searched the want ads for rooms available in downtown Huntington Beach. The downtown area was full of young people, and Main Street consisted of bustling shops on the ground level with bars perched on the second story. If I found a place downtown, I would literally be blocks from the beach. I could walk there, lie in the sand, and study before classes.

I placed phone calls and met with potential roommates, but when they found out that I was primarily a student and only nineteen years old, nobody called me back. No one wanted me as a roommate. I was desperate. Grandma, Grandpa, and Mom were moving in two and a half weeks, and I had nowhere to go. The situation seemed hopeless, and the stress was unbelievable. I was just about to have a mental breakdown when the call finally came.

"Hi, is Amber there?" The voice said. "Yes, this is Amber." "Oh, hi, this is Erica. We met a couple of weeks ago. Are you still interested in renting out the room?" "Yes, absolutely!" *Something must have fallen through with the roommate she really wanted. Why else would she wait two weeks to call me? Aw, who cares, you found a place.* I told myself. And just like that, I became a resident of Downtown Huntington Beach.

Mom stayed primarily with her boyfriend, but still technically lived with Grandma and Grandpa. She packed up and moved from Grandma and Grandpa's first. She bought a one-bedroom condominium. One bedroom! There was no turning back for me. If I failed, there wasn't room at Mom's house for me. Plus, Mom wasn't happy with my decision to part ways with her. A small moving truck arrived, and Grandma and Grandpa helped Mom pack up. I don't remember being there to help. Grandpa and Grandma left a week and a half later, and I watched as their big moving truck made its way out of the cul-de-sac holding all the things I called home. I couldn't help but feel sad and scared. An important chapter was closing, and my safety net was gone. Grandma and Grandpa had seen me through my teenage years. They had watched over and loved me for the last eight years...and now they were gone.

I couldn't move into my new place until the first of the month and had three days to wait it out at the empty house I once called home. I packed my clothes and some miscellaneous belongings into some trash bags. Then I sat in the big empty house and looked around. It was eerie, quiet, and no longer felt like home. The thought of staying the night there alone was frightening, so I stayed with a friend. The following day I went back to the house to get ready for work, but when I turned on the shower, the water never got hot. That night, the electricity was turned off and the house was dark. I was utterly alone; even the house seemed to expel me.

My new room near the beach was slightly larger than a closet. I didn't have any furniture, so its size didn't bother me too much. The furniture in my room at Grandma and Grandpa's house belonged to them. Besides, it wouldn't have fit in my new place anyway. My bedroom furniture from the Cerritos house was long gone. I had nothing. I bought a twin bed for a hundred bucks. It had a pine platform with a green cushion rather than a mattress. It turned into a chair when it was not in use as a bed. I thought that would be convenient for my studies. Then I bought a plastic bin with slide out drawers for my clothes. Voila! My room was complete.

My two new roommates seemed nice but mainly kept to themselves. I had access to the kitchen and living room but did not use either. The house just felt foreign to me. It did not belong to me. Dad came to visit shortly after I moved in. He brought me a laundry basket filled with household items I might need, and we went out to brunch. For the first time ever, Dad really seemed to be there for me. I wanted to rely on him, but he had proven over and over to be unreliable. Shortly after our visit, he sent me a letter.

Hi Am,

I really liked your place. Probably no more than 10% of all the people of the world could live that close to Huntington Beach California. You'll never forget this place. Enjoy! The people will be young and friendly, reminds me of the elite groups of the 60's. They knew how to live and did it!

I'll contact USAA insurance company Monday and have your new policy take affect around the 15th. I will work out a financial pack-age that will give you more money to work with. That's what it's all about huh!

Brunch was pretty overwhelming. I went home and crashed for two or three hours. All my blood rushed to my stomach to digest that

*feast and made me "light headed." Hope you enjoyed the care pack-
age I brought over. I am aware of all the comforts that "Disappear"
when we move; we just got to have them.*

*Work hard to make things happen and they DO! You certainly do
get out of life exactly what you put into it. I'm going to a party next
Saturday (all day). My buddy's employer rents out an entire water
park to show off to their employees. I haven't missed that party for
the last four years! "Eat like Fk'n pigs." All right! I will be thinking of
you working. Sorry about that.*

Hang in there babe. Love ya, Dad

Dad was doing just as he had promised, but I couldn't help but live in
a constant state of anxiety, fearfully waiting for the bottom to drop out.
Certainly, it would, it always did. Would Dad stop sending me the two
hundred dollars rendering me homeless? Would I lose my job? Would I
fail my classes? Would I find someone special in my life? Would I ever get
over Max?

The stress mounted mercilessly. I was never a control freak before but
had suddenly become one. I think I was desperate to create some type of
order, *especially within.*

Several weeks earlier, I had decided part of the reason Max had left was
because I was overweight, ten pounds at least! I fantasized about losing the
weight and prancing around Max in my sexiest outfit. He would rue the
day and surely beg me back. I would delight in his regret and blow him off.
His pain would give me pleasure.

I set in motion an unimaginable, unsustainable diet. I decided I would
eat no more than ten grams of fat per day and not one gram extra! It would
be the low-fat diet of all low-fat diets, and I would not deviate. Baked

potatoes with ketchup on top were pretty filling, or I ate a can of beans. A slice of bread was out of the question. Each slice had at least three grams of fat and I couldn't really make a sandwich anyway because my ten-gram allotment would be reached in one sitting.

I subsisted on rice crackers, saltines, potatoes, and beans. I had long given up red meat, so doing without was easy. Fruit and vegetables were a treat but were not affordable or sustainable. Besides, cooking something wasn't really an option. I didn't feel comfortable using the kitchen at my new place. Often, I skipped breakfast and bought my only meal of the day at Taco Bell, a chicken burrito with no cheese or sauce. My receptionist job had mints on the desk for the customers. Those mints were fat free. So, I would eat those for dinner along with cups of water to fill the void in my stomach. My stomach burned and felt hollow. It felt good.

Over the next few weeks, I watched my frame shrink. My hip bones proudly protruded, and my clothes hung from my frame. My enthusiasm and confidence grew as I shrunk. I was positively empowered by the control I exerted over something...*over me.* I began weighing myself obsessively. I weighed myself when I woke up, and then after I ate. I weighed myself before I pooped, after I pooped. I weighed myself before I exercised, then after. I weighed myself at least ten times a day. Things were spinning out of control fast. Every time someone commented on my weight loss, it bolstered my enthusiasm, and I worked harder to lose more weight.

Within a short time, my body withered away to 98 pounds. Moving into the double digits was a proud moment indeed, but I was starving and soon my enthusiasm was replaced by irritation. Eating disorders are truly reserved for the stubborn and willful, two of my strongest traits. I had successfully created a sickening hybrid disorder complete with deprivation, some bulimia, obsessive weigh-ins, and food destruction...*Yes, I said it... food destruction.*

My relationship with food became very personal. Food dictated my moods, which were mostly sad and angry. The first time it happened in public at a restaurant. I was so hungry and deprived I decided I would finally allow myself a normal meal. Well, sort of: I ordered the club sandwich with no bacon, cheese, or mayo. The picture on the menu made the sandwich look heavenly. It had lettuce and tomato hanging over the edges and was piled high with turkey.

My mouth watered and my mind acquiesced. *I was in charge here, and today, I was going to eat that sandwich. It was going to come out on a dish looking just as it did in the picture on the menu, gloriously thick with lots of lettuce.* All I could think about was that sandwich, but when the waitress finally delivered it before me, I was disgusted. The sandwich she delivered was far from perfect. It was not lightly toasted, there was barely any lettuce on it, and it was certainly not piled high with turkey. It was nothing like the god damned picture and I wanted nothing to do with that sad, miserable sandwich.

I was so disappointed and angry that tears formed and I had to excuse myself, leaving my date sitting there baffled. Surely, he thought I was insane. I went to the bathroom and sobbed. *I would not eat that poor excuse for a sandwich and derail my progress. That sandwich was NOT worth it!* I returned to the table after composing myself and did not eat the sandwich. Instead, I systematically disassembled the sandwich and moved it around the plate. Then, I used my fork to stab and smash it. Hurting that sandwich felt good.

Despite being hungry as hell, I refused to give up the strange control and continued to obsessively adhere to this punishing diet. I was with several friends having dinner one night when I embarrassed myself completely. I ordered the grilled cheese sandwich. The picture on the menu depicted a thick sandwich with cheese oozing out the sides. I decided to allow the sandwich just this once. I wouldn't eat a thing the next day.

The sandwich arrived on two flimsy pieces of white bread and the processed cheese still lay in the middle barely melted. I was furious. *Damn it! I would not eat this sandwich!* Then I clenched my fist and hammered away at the sandwich over and over, punishing it for disappointing me so thoroughly. I smashed the thing until it was unrecognizable, and when I finally looked up from my plate my friends sat staring, their mouths agape. *Christ, it was official, I had gone quite mad…over a grilled cheese sandwich!* The looks on my friends' faces were undeniable: *shock.* I had even managed to shock myself. *Something had to give…something had to fill this void.*

CHAPTER 16

Enter Dean, my hero

Adam graduated from college and married his college sweetheart, Debra. A short time later, he became a dad. When Adam's first son was born, he sang me his favorite song by R.E.M: "It's the end of the world as we know it and I feel fine." Adam was happy and indeed, was going to be just fine.

I began dating soon after Max broke up with me, but no one fulfilled me in the sick way that he had. A couple of months after the breakup, I was at a friend's house in Huntington Beach celebrating the Fourth of July, when I peered down from the balcony and saw Dean in a sea of people. I had just turned twenty and my life was about to get a whole lot better.

Dean had bleached blond hair, blue eyes, tan skin, and shared Dad's name… *Dean.* Lucky for me, that irony was the only commonality they shared. Dean had chicken legs and a really nice ass, which somehow held up his heaving muscular top half. His back was wide and his chest and arms bulged with lean muscle. I had met Dean four years earlier, when I was sixteen. He was Max's older brother's buddy. I had a little crush on him then and thought he was adorably funny, but I was already in a relationship with Max.

The timing was finally right, and God had placed him right before me…his apparent offering for all my suffering. Dean resisted temptation the entire day, rebuffing my embarrassingly forward come-ons. He repeatedly told me that I had dated Max and that he should not get involved with me, but I was unrelenting and totally took advantage of his intoxicated state. When he finally kissed me that day, I knew he was the one.

Dean was sensitive and pensive. He was responsible beyond his years; he had two jobs and wanted to become a fireman. No saving for me to do here. Maybe he was my hero…maybe I was the one in need of saving.

We began dating exclusively, and our relationship grew. We spent all our time together, and I told him my secrets. My problems with food seemed to vanish. I told Dean all about Dad and he just laughed. He thought Dad sounded funny and was eager to meet him. No amount of preparation could ever suffice to mitigate the shock he was in for. I tried to hold off introductions as long as possible, but when Adam's first son was born, I knew I needed to travel to San Diego with Dean to see the baby and inevitably, Dad would be there.

We arrived in San Diego and Dad was already drunk. He was an amateur drinker. It was not his vice of first choice, and he could never hold his liquor. *At least he wasn't high on drugs*, I thought. "Hey *grandpa*," I teased sarcastically. "Don't call me *grandpa*, call me Papa Dean" Dad said proudly. "Papa Dean, huh? That has a nice ring, I like it" I said.

Dad was in rare form. He was wildly manic, talking a mile a minute while he took pictures holding the baby. Not normal pictures but his usual inappropriate awful stuff: him holding the baby's middle finger up or holding his lit cigarette near the baby's face as if he were already smoking. Dean looked at me with wide eyes, obviously shocked by "The Dad Show." I spent two hours in the car driving to San Diego giving Dean blow by blow examples of the shock he would be in for, but nothing could assuage the grossly offensive events that were about to play out.

Dad was out of booze and insisted that Dean accompany him to the liquor store. He was even going to drive…poor Dean. God knows what was said during their car ride, but Dean did return in one piece, shell-shocked. I got him alone to find out what happened, and he sputtered that Dad had a number of air-horns in his vehicle, which he deployed randomly, scaring the shit out of unsuspecting pedestrians. Then once they got into the liquor store, he feared they might be shot when Dad went behind the counter to inspect the Butterscotch Schnapps up close and personal. When the cashier freaked out and told him he could not be behind the counter in his area, Dad verbally chastised the man and told him to "get his shit together and to refrigerate the Schnapps in the future!"

Dean quickly began to realize what we were dealing with here…a *special brand of crazy*. The rest of the day played out just as I knew it would, one shocking revelation after the next with Dad's vulgar mouth and inappropriate behavior. I was used to it and embarrassment had long given way to exasperation, but this was new to Dean, and Dad was on a mission to fully indoctrinate him.

On the way home from San Diego, Dad rode behind us in his truck arms flailing while he laid on four different air-horns, each with their uniquely annoying sound. Dean had gotten used to the sounds of the air horns, but before long Dad began bumping our vehicle from behind as we traveled down the freeway. Knowing that the situation was dangerous, I pulled off the freeway and talked Dad into going to eat at a nearby Mexican restaurant.

We arrived at the restaurant, and Dad's antics continued. He flirted with the heavy-set waitress and flipped up her little ruffled skirt as she walked away. I shrank down in my seat wondering what he would do next. Dad had just gotten dentures. He insisted that the dentist extract the remainder of his teeth, even the good ones. The dentist advised Dad against it, but he demanded his teeth be pulled. He was plain tired of them! Unused to how his new dentures felt in his mouth, they flopped all around and gave him a lisp I had never heard before. Dad usually ate like a barbarian, and the fear that he might take his dentures out prior to the meal made me flush with anxiety.

The meal arrived, and the waitress warned us all of the hot plates as she gingerly set them in front of us. Dad grasped the fork in his entire palm, "prison style," and took a heaping scoop of beans, which strung molten hot cheese from the plate all the way up to his mouth. He gasped for air as the beans and his teeth fell out of his mouth and yelled, "You said the plate was hot, not the beans!"

Dean and I had been dating for six months when things started getting serious. We lived two blocks from one another, but I began spending the night at his house most days of the week, abandoning the lonely room I had rented. Dean lived with his older brother and another roommate, and they did a good job tolerating my constant presence. But before long, they tired of our public displays of affection in the living room, and they protested one evening by marching downstairs in their underwear. Dean was positively offended, but it went right over my head. Dad routinely traipsed around the house in his skivvies, and I had no idea Dean's roommates were attempting to "make a statement."

Dean and I soon realized that finding our own place was necessary, and we began searching for an apartment of our own. Mom and Dad were thrilled about the prospect of us cohabitating, while Dean's conservative folks were less than excited. Despite their disapproval, the search was unrelenting and before long we found a one-bedroom, one-bathroom apartment a couple of blocks away from Dean's apartment for $650.00 a month. We moved in together, and for the first time in a very long time, a happy satisfaction settled over me. Indeed, I would marry Dean. He was my hero.

I continued working thirty hours a week and transferred to a State University. Meanwhile, Dean worked full time, volunteered at a local fire department, and tested fervently to become a paid fireman. In short order, we learned to work together toward mutual goals. I graduated with a bachelor's degree in 1996 and applied with a local probation department. I had spent an inordinate amount of time over the years attempting to change those around me. Maybe working in probation would be different. The background check was lengthy, so in the meantime, I got a job at a group home working with severely emotionally disturbed adolescents. *Funny, how I sought out chaos when it wasn't present.*

My first day at the group home I was instructed to "get to know" the fifteen girls who lived in one half of the residence. It really wasn't a residence at all. It was an old psychiatric hospital that had been converted into "a home" for kids who had entered the Social Services system. They called the home a "Level 14" facility, and I was told the kids who lived there required the "highest level of service." Foster homes were out of the question because these kids were not adoptable. They were heavily medicated and virtually beyond repair. One half of the facility housed young girls, while the other half housed young boys. This sad place was their home.

I watched in horror as the day and each of the residents completely unraveled. I should have immediately known what I was in for when one of the young girls approached me and said, "You know, you really should wear your hair in a braid or ponytail, because when I *go off*, I pull hair." Before lunch, I participated in the restraint of an unruly 13-year-old and witnessed another one of the girls assault a staff member. My new coworkers were actually surprised when I returned from my lunch break.

For nearly one year, I went to work in absolute chaos, and frighteningly, I adapted somewhat naturally. Dad's crazy behavior must have prepared me for chaos, because nothing seemed to shock me. Apparently, like Mom, I had become far more adaptable than most. When one of the residents chased me through the house threatening to hurl his feces my way, I ran and dodged the bullet. I didn't quit. When a kid grabbed me from behind and held Plexi-glass to my throat, I talked him out of doing anything stupid. I didn't quit. One of the kids routinely held a spoon in his hand and told me he planned to "scoop my eye out," but I kept showing up for work. I was assaulted daily but no amount of abuse deterred me.

I was working with an antisocial population…similar to Dad, but with far better excuses; these kids had actually been victimized. I read each child's file…detailed accounts of the unimaginable. Some of the stories were so horrific and heartbreaking; I actually felt pain in the center of my chest. One 12-year-old boy was used as a human ashtray, while another wore scars on his face from scalding water. Some were abused for years, not only by their parents but by a host of derelicts their parent failed to protect them from. The thing that astonished me more than reading about a human being capable of dishing out such abuse was the ability of a child to completely forgive. Children love unconditionally. Despite the abuse these kids endured, they possessed a love so primal for their parent that they would sooner take the abuse than be separated from their abuser. I completely understood, having lived with Dad for all those years.

Monday 11/25/1996

Dear Amber-- Sweet cheeks, hard body, bay watch babe,

Sometimes we neglect ourselves. When I don't write you enough let-
ters, I neglect me too. Sorry Amber. That will be the purpose of this
fine note then-- OK? We've all worked hard to finish up the year and
should be rewarded greatly! No? You push your parents and I'll push
mine for these rewards. I've always been able to do better than you
in that area! I'm not at all afraid about talking money with anyone.
It's just part of life that needs to be well planned to be successful and
some of the best plans get SQUASHED in the end. We'll all make
it ...friends and family anyhow...we can't save the whole world.
So, congratulations on your long ass haul through to receive your
Bachelor's Degree. You'll find it hard to believe too! What now? No
more classes? I'm not ready yet? I don't know that much yet! Get a
job? The related fields of study may not pay shit to start out with.
You're a freshman all over again. Everyone applying for your job has
a degree too. Even a Master's degree. Better look for something that
really interests you. You won't dwell on a lack of money that you
receive for your services in the beginning. Build up takes time and
experience, and hard work, no matter what field of expertise you
choose. Thus, ends my thoughts for tonight C-ya babe, love ya, Dad.

CHAPTER 17

I think there are two types of people in this world

I think there are two types of people in this world. The type who runs out the day after their dog dies to buy a puppy to soften the hurt *or* the type who vows never again to own a dog. Mom falls into the second category. She never married again after Dad. She gave him so much of her heart there was not enough left for anyone else.

Dad seemed to be in good spirits. He seemed to have more clarity. I even wondered for a moment if he was sober. I inquired, "what's going on Dad, you seem mighty happy and focused lately."

"There is someone I want you to meet!" Dad said.

"Really, who?" I asked

"A lady friend."

"Oh really…what's her name…when can I meet her?"

"Donna…How about this Saturday, we can get a bite to eat."

I met Dad at the restaurant and saw a young woman standing next to him. *That couldn't be her, she was my age,* I thought.

"Hey Am!"

"Hey pops!"

"This is Donna."

"Hi, nice to meet you Donna." *Was he actually dating this girl? What could she possibly want with Dad?*

"How old are you Donna?"

"Twenty-four."

I jerked my head toward Dad and sarcastically retorted, "Interesting, that's my brother's age."

"I know," she replied smiling.

The lunch wore on, and as much as I would have liked to antagonize the girl and say mean-spirited things to drive her away…I couldn't. I liked her. I felt a little sorry for her. There was no way she would be able to manage Dad…*no one could.* She was so young and naïve. She had no clue what she was in for.

Dad was smitten with Donna, and within a year they married. Contentment seemed to settle over Dad for a time, but it didn't last. They divorced after a year or so. Dad told me he got into a fight after Donna went to a concert with a friend and came home drunk. I will never know the entire story or what trials Donna endured. She left Dad never to re-emerge. I wondered if she was as wounded as Dad. Dad's inability to impose himself on her *will* and conquer her completely tormented him. I think this may have been the first time he experienced rejection and the heartache that comes with loving someone who does not love you in return. Dad said years later, "Now I know how your Mom felt." His comment actually surprised and disappointed me. He really didn't know how Mom felt when they divorced; he didn't share her heartbreak at the time.

Dean and I had been living together for two years and were hopelessly in love. We talked about marriage and knew it was in our future. I wanted Dean to propose to me with the antique ring Grandma had given me years earlier. It was dainty and made of platinum with small stones carefully set around a star sapphire. My hope was that Dean would replace the sapphire with a diamond when he finally popped the question. I told him, "When you decide it is time, this is the ring I'd like." Dean dutifully took the ring and plopped it in a jar of pennies he was collecting. It sat there untouched for over a year. Every time a special day approached, be it Christmas, an anniversary, or my birthday, I would sneak over to the penny jar to see if my platinum ring still lay among the copper...and there it sat.

When Valentine's Day approached, I peered into the jar; yep, still there. *Damn it Dean!* You can imagine my surprise when he came home after work, got on his knee in our apartment's small kitchen, and asked me to marry him. No ring…just a single red rose in his hand.

I had always pictured my wedding in Mama Brown's backyard. Her home, particularly the backyard, was the backdrop for happy childhood memories, a place where family celebrated the holidays and other special occasions. It sat perched on a hill of its own in La Habra Heights and over-looked the entire Los Angeles Valley below. On a clear day, you could see all the way to Catalina Island, and at night the city lights twinkled as far as the eye could see.

I didn't know how to ask Grandma for such a huge favor…I didn't want to ask. *I hated asking for help.* I rarely resorted to requesting aid. Like Mom, adapting to circumstance was my forte; the alternative really screwed with my pride. I flushed when imagining grandma's regretful decline … *"Sorry honey, that isn't going to work."*

I needed Dad to talk to Grandma, but I wasn't sure how he would respond to such a request either. He would only ask her if he sanctioned the idea. Over the years, I learned that Dad didn't really want to be asked to do anything…making him believe it was his idea achieved far better results. I took a trip to grandma's house to show her and Dad the ring. Dean and I had just replaced the sapphire with a diamond, and the engagement finally felt real. I carefully selected my words and when I got Dad alone I said, "Dad, wouldn't it be awesome if Dean and I got married right here in the backyard?" And just like that, Dad made it happen…it was his doing; he liked it best that way.

"June 21st" That's the day! The first day of summer and the longest day of the year…it's perfect!" I pictured myself in a long white dress making my way down an isle toward Grandma's gazebo. Dean and I had a little over a year to plan the details of our wedding and we already knew it would take place in Grandma's backyard. Not only was Dad able to convince Grandma that her house would make a perfect backdrop for the wedding, but he handed over five thousand dollars toward expenses.

We went to Grandma's house and looked around the big yard. "Okay, we can put the dance floor over here and the food over there," I said smiling. Dean pointed out the dead grass and overgrown weeds and asked, "Are you sure you want to get married here?" I'm sure" I said, ignoring the obstacles. "This yard can easily hold two hundred people." I said excitedly. Dean quickly brought me back down to earth, "What bathrooms are these two hundred people using Amber? Your Grandma's house is on a septic tank! Plus, how is anyone going to see each other back here? There are no lights!" "Jeez, Dean, it will work out! We can rent outhouses and put candles on the tables." "Outhouses?" He scoffed. "Ya, I bet they make nice ones for stuff like this. I know they do! I have been in outhouses with sinks in them and everything!" I said.

"Where is everyone going to park Amber? There isn't enough room on the hill for all those cars." "They can park at the bottom of the hill." I said exasperated. "Then what…walk up that huge hill in their dress clothes?" "Damn it Dean, if you don't want to get married here, why don't' you just say so!" "Sweetie, I do, but you need to think about all of the logistics." "We'll, work it out, it's do-able. We can get a van and hire someone to chauffer people up the hill." I said with impossible optimism. Dean's voice became serious, "Honey, this is going to cost a lot more than we expected."

Dean was right and I knew it. It would be a costly logistical nightmare. I sat contemplating the hurdles and grimaced. Then Dean said, "Oh babe, you are right, we have plenty of time to iron out the wrinkles, it will be great."

Two months later, I ignored the obvious problems and found a catering company ten minutes from Grandma's house. I reserved the date, ordered Mexican food for two hundred, and wrote a check for the deposit in the amount of two thousand dollars-- a pretty good chunk of our budget.

Dad liked the idea of a wedding on his turf. He was excited. "You watch Amber, this yard is going to be awesome," he said. Dad could talk Grandma into anything and must have gotten right to work. As the wedding date approached, giant light posts were erected, and a carpet of sod was rolled out. Grandma even built a beautiful fountain. It seemed that everything was working out.

Monday, 4/28/1997

Hi Amber and Dean,

I have the maps for your wedding invitations and will take it early Monday to the typesetter. Please be OK with Papa Brown's untimely passing. He is in shut down and refuses food. All funeral arrangements have been made in advance. Mama Brown is OK with this. I took her to dinner at Red Lobster and had a shrimp feast Sunday night and spent the night with her up there at the house. Please call your mom and prepare her-- best possible results. Papa Brown is in no pain. Alicia and you cannot allow this to bring you down before your weddings. It's his time very soon and it is OK. Get strong and prepare for better times ahead of us NOW. All is well and that's the way it should be...hold on guys, hold on to each other. I am more concerned for your feelings than Papa Brown's. He's OK with this too! Believe me. Love ya, Dad

My sweet Grandpa Brown passed away the night Dad took Grandma to the Red Lobster. Dad wrote and mailed my letter the following morning before learning this news. Grandpa had been suffering from Alzheimer's disease for so long. Grandma had dutifully cared for him for the last ten years before he finally passed. I felt sad knowing Grandpa would not see me get married in his yard, but he had left us all a long time ago anyway.

My cousin got married in May, a month before my wedding was to take place. She was married on a bluff overlooking the ocean, but despite the gorgeous venue, I couldn't help but sense a strange tension. I pulled my cousin's sister aside and asked, "What's wrong?" "Well, our fathers decided to have a threesome with the maid of honor last night. My mother could hear them screwing through the hotel walls all night." My mouth fell open and suddenly I realized something I had failed to consider. *How was Dad going to behave on my wedding day?* Shortly after my cousin's wedding, I received another letter from Dad.

Hello Amber,

Sure was a fun party at Alisha's wedding and reception huh? WORE ME OUT, but the most fun was being with you. Deanie is a lucky man. I sure the fuck hope he knows what he really has here. You need only have a few bad ones to be able to recognize a jewel when you see it! Adam and Deb are also valuable people. I don't deserve this impressive of a family. Not from what I've had to work with! I came home early Sunday morning (2 am) after I woke up from my basic hangover... I was only a 20-minute drive away? Your people will know how important they are when they come to your well-planned wedding in June. No? Lots of stuff came together, because lots of people cared to make it happen. Wasn't your mama, Juicy Joycie, cutting it up on the dance floor? Glad to see that she can still generate that "wild gear." Joyce agreed to a "Finland Trip" with me in 1998-- not now. She won't admit it to anyone I'm sure, but that's OK with me. I'll preserve her integrity too and only tell you! I'm OK with wanting her back. I see we fit too well to have undone in the first place. And I told her that too, as I forgave all my other fuck ups.

I think your uncle is through with "tag teams." This woman was too wild for him. He couldn't wear her out as quickly as he once thought. She wasn't your "standard quitter" but wasn't anything unusual either. "We did good, Jerry" I said…we sent her home to her family where she belongs in the first place. Margaret, Erin, and Alisha were in the NEXT ROOM! They did not make friendly advances, but they did admit to staying up ALL NIGHT LONG! Hum?? I don't regret a thing. Guess they picked the wrong bridesmaid this trip. If it wasn't us it would have been four other people! No? That's how many we needed in the room! C ya, Love ya, Dad.

Three weeks before our wedding day, Dean and some of his friends went up to Grandma's house to string white lights on the hillside and in the trees. Grandma contacted the neighbor below who had equestrian property, and they agreed to allow our guests to park in their stable area. Dean reserved a fifteen-passenger van and hired two drivers to take people up Grandma's steep driveway. He also managed to find two decent outhouses for the occasion. *We were really going to pull this thing off.*

"Don't worry about the kegs. I will handle that detail. I know the guy at the liquor store right down the hill." Dad boasted. "Okay, Dad, but that is an important detail. We don't want to run out of booze!" "Worry about nothing Am, I got it covered." The rehearsal dinner took place the day before the wedding. Butterflies danced around in my stomach as my bridesmaids arranged themselves beside me. The minister went through the ceremony, and I glanced over to see Dad standing there, watching. He had a look of pride I had never quite seen before. *I wondered if he thought about his wedding day. The first one…the only one that mattered.*

That night, we all gathered in the yard to turn on the lights we had strung weeks earlier. "One, two, three…." The lights came on and lit the yard up like Disneyland. We all stood and marveled at the beauty. Then suddenly, the lights went off…all of them…even the ones in the house. "Oh my god, what happened? I think I'm going to be sick!" I moaned. "Don't worry Ambie, it's probably just a fuse…we'll fix it, no big deal," my old friend Becky said in her usual comforting way. I don't know what I worried about more…losing power during the wedding or Dad embarrassing me. It was probably a tie, but the second was the more likely of the two.

The following day I watched as the chairs were placed in rows surrounding Grandma's gazebo. Pink flowers graced the façade of the gazebo, and tables lined the perimeter of the hill overlooking the valley…just as I had imagined. I stood a while watching the table linens blow in the breeze and was suddenly overtaken by peace. *Nothing could ruin this day…I was about to marry my hero.*

Dad was so excited. He came bounding into the room where I was getting ready and gave me a big hug. "You look beautiful! What a gorgeous dress!" "Dad, this is my bra and slip!" I laughed. "Well, maybe you should wear that, it's stunning!" Just then, the photographer came in and started taking pictures. Apparently, he too thought I was dressed.

"Jeez guys… let me get dressed!" I hollered, ushering them out. I hadn't seen Dean all morning. I wondered what he was up to. My buddy and old roommate Erica, who I had lived with so long ago in Huntington Beach, came into the room with a sober look on her face. I had appointed her my "Wedding Nazi," and she was taking the job seriously.

"This is for you…it's from Dean." She said handing me a letter. I carefully tore open the envelope and found Dean's familiar handwriting.

Amber, June 21, 1997

Well, it's finally here. All of our planning and organizing will come together today. I just want you to know how much I love you and how important this day is to me. We have been through a lot together and we will go through a lot more, but no matter what, I will always be by your side.

The ring that I put on today will not just be a decoration, but a symbol of our love and life together. I will wear it with pride and dignity. When we are apart, I will look at it and think of you and all the love I feel for you.

We are now officially starting our family and that will be my number one priority for now and forever. Thank you for being you. I love you with all my heart and soul. We will have a wonderful life together. See you at 6:00 pm. Love, Dean

Erica ran in to collect me at 6:00. "It's time!" The music sounded and I watched as my best friends walked arm and arm with Dean's best friends around the corner and out of sight. I looked at Dad in his tuxedo and fresh haircut. He wore pride well and looked so handsome. Dad gave me a knowing smile, then walked me down the aisle, kissed me on the cheek, and gave me away to Dean. He sat down next to Mom and held her hand through the entire ceremony. Dad always said he lived with no regrets, but

I know this wasn't entirely true. Dad behaved like a perfect gentleman the entire night, surprising even me. Every time I looked over at him, I saw that twinkle in his eye and marveled at his restraint.

CHAPTER 18

Triple Crown Winner

Dean and I met Dad for breakfast at a coffee shop. He was *high* and much more animated than usual. I shrank down in my seat hoping others would not pay any mind to the way he contorted and wriggled in his seat, but that hope gave way when a flow of blood spontaneously poured from his nose.

"You are my *Triple Crown Winner* Am." Dad said. "Triple Crown Winner?" I asked. "Yep, you walked for graduation, Cum Laude, I might add, got married, and got deputized all in the same year. What a feat!" "Yes, I guess you are right pops. Crazy, all that has happened huh?" Right after Dean and I got married, I was hired by the Probation Department as a Deputy Juvenile Correction Officer. Simultaneously, Dean was hired as a Firefighter. Dean and I made a powerful team, and our hard work was finally starting to pay off.

I was assigned to Juvenile Hall and planned to save the world one kid at a time. A girl named Denise was assigned to train me. "Okay, you never want to go into a room if there is a kid in there. NEVER! When you do your "room shakedowns" make sure to always "key back" the door-- this disengages the locking mechanism. If you don't do that, the lock is still engaged and a kid can walk by, shut the door, and you will be locked in there."

I looked down at the keys that hung from my utility belt. These were no ordinary keys. They were huge and heavy, color-coded and complicated. I rubbed the bottle of pepper spray attached to my belt and wondered if I would ever need to use it.

"Now, be on the lookout for contraband and weapons. The kids aren't allowed to have any hygiene items in their rooms because they sharpen their toothbrushes and use them as shanks. You will always find a *Fifi Bag* or two...fucking disgusting." "Fifi Bag?" I asked. "Oh, you don't know about *Fifi* yet?" Denise laughed heartily. "Well, the kids make vaginas out of anything they can find. They get downright creative too. Usually, you will just find a glove tied off, but sometimes, they'll straight up make a hole in their mattress, dig the stuffing out, and shove their dicks in there."

I cringed. "Jesus, that's gross. What do you mean I will find a tied-off glove? Do I give them consequences for that?" "Oh, the kids are always trying to get a hold of the staff's plastic gloves. They steal them during

Saturday morning cleanup all the time. They put lotion in those things then screw them. Pretty easy cleanup…the cum goes in the glove and then they tie it off. They try to throw them away in the morning but have to be sneaky about it because they know they aren't supposed to bring any trash out of their room at that time."

"When can they throw trash away?" I asked. "When you do last head calls at 9:30 pm. Oh, another thing…if you see them jerking off during your room checks, yell at them and tell them to knock it off. If you don't, they'll think you're okay with that, and rest assured, all the kids will beat their meat on your shift…one big fucking circle jerk."

"Are you serious?" I asked. "Serious as a heart attack. That idiot who works in unit G wears perfume and gets gussied up to come to this place. The boys love her. They wait till she comes in for her shift and sit facing the window while they play with their balls. It freaks her out so bad that she doesn't even confront them…she just ignores it, like it's not even happening. So, listen to me, okay? Kick their door when you see that behavior and tell them to put that little thing back in their pants. They won't ever do it again around you."

I walked by a room, and a gangster type smirked at me through the window. Then down the long hallway the cat calls began, "SHEEEOW! HEEEY MISSUS WHITE!" *I cringed and thought: what had I gotten myself into?"*

I had a surprise party for Dean's 30th birthday: a Cinco de Mayo themed party with Mexican food and a huge cooler full of beer. I sent Dean off that day to play golf with his dad, and when he returned home a slew of friends were waiting to yell, "Surprise!" I wore a tight black halter dress for the occasion, which Dean seemed very impressed with. That night we hung from the rafters. We celebrated into the early morning hours and still didn't want the party to end. "Don't leave, have another taquito," I slurred as our friends stumbled away.

The next morning, I paid for drinking all that beer. Dean and I went to our favorite place for breakfast, but when the food came, I thought I would vomit. "I feel sick Dean, take me home." Two days later, I still felt crummy, and that is when I realized my period was days late. I had stopped taking my birth control pill a year earlier in an attempt to get pregnant, but nothing had happened. Dean and I both expected that I would get pregnant within a couple of months but were sorely disappointed ten months in a row. Honestly, we had just started to worry whether something was wrong.

I had a stash of pregnancy tests in the bathroom cupboard. I had even saved a couple of used ones hoping the bad news on the stick might change. Dean waited outside the bathroom as I carefully unwrapped the long package and urinated on the familiar end. *Come on, damn it!* Dean and I sat and watched as the little stick foretold our future. I was finally pregnant! "Let me pee on another one just to make sure!" I squealed. We were overjoyed. Our family was about to expand. That November, I went into pre-mature labor and delivered our first precious son nine weeks early. Conner weighed a mere four pounds and remained in the hospital for a solid month. As he lay helpless in his incubator, I stared at his tiny features wondering what the future would hold for him and who he would take after. I felt a love so strong, that I could only describe it as being *Godly*. And when I believed I could not ever possibly feel a love this intense, it happened again two years later, when I gave birth to my second treasured son, Carson.

I was working in unit S at Juvenile Hall when my belly started to protrude. I had been working in the institution for two years and was comfortable with its eccentricities.

Here's a rundown of my day: *"When your doors open, put your shoes on inside your room, then stand outside your door and wait for instructions. Your rooms should be in room inspection order with your blankets folded."* I yell. I walk down the long hallway to supervise "line movement" as my coworker stands at the desk operating the doors and I yell, *"Pop one through ten!"* Instantly, ten doors on the right side of the hallway open. My heavy keys clang against my hip as I walk down the hallway. *"Line up gentlemen and take it down the hall to the bathroom. Use it if you need to and then have a seat in the carpet area."* A group of boys walk silently down the hallway with their hands behind their back and their heads cast down. *"Mrs. White, can I …."* *"No questions right now Rodriguez, save it for the carpet area,"* I say.

I walk behind the group, watching their every move. Four male juveniles filter into the bathroom as I stand there to supervise "stand ups and sit downs." The smell of excrement wafts out of the bathroom, and a loud fart echoes in the porcelain bowl. The bathroom erupts in laughter. *"Cut it out gentlemen. Take care of your business and get to the carpet area for structure…wash your hands Rodriguez."* *"Pop eleven through eighteen!"* Pop, Pop, Pop…and more of the same. I had become Mom. Order felt nice.

"Gentlemen, if you do not know me, my name is Mrs. White. I will be here today until 10:00 pm. If you are following the rules and doing as you're told, we will have a good day together. If you are acting up, you will find yourself in your room come free time tonight. We will be going out for LME momentarily—Large Muscle Exercise. I have handballs, and you may play basketball. If you don't get along with someone, stay away from them. If I need to talk to you about your behavior, you are probably going to wind up

in your room. I brought a movie and some popcorn tonight, so let's have a good day. Don't blow it...any questions?" "What movie did you bring Mrs. White?" "Hopefully, you will be one of the gentlemen out for free time tonight to find out Rodriguez."

Working in an institution changed me. Not immediately, but over the years, I had become somewhat jaded. I knew full well the evil that man was capable of. The murderers I dealt with weren't even men, just 16- and 17-year-old boys. I had become exhausted seeing the same kids get released only to return over and over. It seemed futile, as monotonous as the rules I robotically parroted every day. I wasn't making any positive change. What I was doing didn't seem to help a damn bit. My nightly group counseling that I poured my heart into seemed useless. *Maybe like Dad, they liked the life they chose....*

After five years working as a correctional officer at Juvenile Hall and when I thought I might not be able to endure the disappointment of my toiling any longer, I was finally promoted to a field assignment as a probation officer. I was excited again. Maybe this assignment would be different. Maybe I could really help people make positive changes in their lives. With a renewed sense of purpose, my "I can save the world" attitude seemed restored to its college-day fervor. The last day of my probation officer academy we all sat holding our breath waiting for our assignments. "Sherry, you will be going to adult field supervision, John, juvenile field supervision. Mike, you are going to be assigned to adult Harbor Court. Amber, you will be at Juvenile Hall, Custody Intake...." The instructors droned on handing out assignments, but all I heard was *Juvenile Hall*. Christ, I had just come from there, it had nearly beaten me down and now I was required to return? That smelly sad place wanted to finish me off.

For me, disappointment was always a short-lived emotion. *Optimism,* I would learn, was my saving grace. It was the special quality or gene that carried me through life's tragedies and had on many occasions made me oblivious to the bleakness of my situation. *There's a reason I'm going back to the institution, I thought. I just don't know what that reason is yet.*

My new assignment required me to complete Detention Reports for every child booked into Juvenile Hall. Additionally, I was tasked with interviewing juveniles and their parents in order to complete Pretrial Reports for the court. Working at Juvenile Hall all those years gave me enormous perspective into the minds of the kids housed there, but I had little to no insight about their parents, the people who had unsuccessfully reared them. How did these kids get to this horrible crossroad? *Were their fathers just like Dad?*

I had interviewed a couple hundred separate families, when I discovered the answer as to why these kids behaved the way they did. It came as no surprise and was just as I suspected: 85% of the time, the blame lay with the parents. They enabled their kids, made excuses for them, and even lied for them. They spoiled them and let them run amok with no consistent boundaries. They befriended their children in a destructive way, partying with them and even shared their drugs.

It was the same story, over and over again; a different set of parents but the same damn story. I started keeping notes to detail the patterns so clearly responsible for the failure of these youth. I needed to play a bigger part in the solution, and the bureaucracy I worked for seemed slow and scared to take risks. My frustration was funneled into pages and pages of hand-written thoughts detailing the factors contributing to juvenile delinquency. My heart went out to each parent I interviewed. I wholeheartedly understood their sorrow, confusion, and frustration. During this process, I couldn't help but to contemplate my own impossible childhood...*I had absolutely beat the odds.* Having children of my own brought things closer to home. How terrible to lose a child to drugs or the streets. I truly sympathized with the parents I interviewed. The sad truth was, I couldn't help but to think about my own gene pool. What if that shitty gene skipped a generation again and landed in my own offspring? I had dodged a bullet, but would my children be predisposed? Is there truly a genetic component with the "Nature versus Nurture" theory? If I better understood what made people take the wrong fork in the road, maybe then I could prevent delinquency and other antisocial behavior.

A year and a half into my writing, I realized I had finished my first book. A parenting book sarcastically entitled "How to Raise a Juvenile Delinquent: A Common Sense Approach to Parenting." My optimism triumphed over circumstance, and although Dad was my biggest saboteur I couldn't help but give him some credit him for my success. I dreamed big ...just like Dad. He made me believe that anything was possible.

A book signing event marked the birth of my accomplishment. I was a published author, and a part of me believed that my book finally signified solid proof that indeed, I was intelligent...something I had questioned and underestimated since being overlooked by that god-damned "MGM" program in elementary school. The publication celebration was a classy affair: wine, hors d'oeuvres, flowers, and an ice sculpture. I wore a black dress, and my hair sat neatly piled on top of my head in a sophisticated hairdo. I don't remember ever feeling so proud of myself. Even my inner voice, the doubter who routinely minimized and dismissed my successes, kept her mouth shut.

I was signing books when I saw Dad walk in and my heart dropped. He wore his favorite stained dinner jacket and looked skinnier than usual. His cheeks looked rather concave, and his skin looked mottled and unhealthy. But his general disheveled appearance was not what caused the wave of embarrassment to turn my ears crimson. I was certain he was *high*. I furtively looked around trying to gauge the reaction of my guests. Over the years, I had spent a great deal of time scrutinizing Dad's body language to determine whether he was under the influence of drugs. There were unmistakable telltale signs such as the way his legs bounced up and down when he was seated, the way his jaw clenched, and his body contorted unnaturally, and the way he'd ramble on.

Most of the time, Dad's drug use was abundantly obvious because he made no effort to conceal it. Sometimes, he'd even pull the bag of white powder from his shirt pocket and flick it with his finger as he smiled devilishly. I would always shake my head in disapproval, but what could I do? He bragged about his indiscretions, and after a while I stopped chastising him because I knew nothing was going to change. I had no control over Dad and I accepted this fact. I imagine his flagrancy was an effort to somehow include me in his guilt and force me to share his culpability. He wanted to mitigate and legitimize his wrongdoing.

Whether Dad boasted about or concealed his cocaine use, I didn't like the person he became when he was high. That person wasn't my Dad; he was an imposter and any interactions with him were disingenuous. Of course, he would always argue that the behavior was 100% him, drugs or no drugs. Dad's reality left me questioning the truth, feeling uncertain and distrustful. His truth was simply not reality.

Dad bought a dozen of my books and had me autograph them all. Pride just oozed from him. His approval was very gratifying, but I was humiliated. I was ashamed of my Dad... and more ashamed of myself for feeling that way. Dad was a drug addict, and I did not want everyone to know. I had kept this fact a secret from many people, fearful that I would be cast in the same negative light. For some reason, I believed I was an extension of Dad, a reflection of him. His foibles and embarrassments were not his alone. I shared them and took them on as my own. *I suspect most enablers do....*

I sat contemplating my shame, wondering if anyone else realized that Dad had shown up to my special event *high*. That fact certainly did not escape my inner doubter, who heckled, *"Wait till everyone finds out the author of a parenting book was raised by a drug addict...that ought to lend credibility."*

CHAPTER 19

Dad led a messy life. No wonder Mom was always cleaning

I remember eating sunflower seeds at Dad's house when I was about fourteen years old. I was seated on the couch and had carefully piled the empty shells on a napkin beside me. Dad came by and said, "You don't have to do that, I have a great vacuum, just spit your seeds right onto the floor." Then Dad smacked the pile of seeds right off the napkin, strewing them all over the floor. We sat there for about an hour spitting the seeds everywhere, laughing. Dad led a messy life and liked it best that way. *No wonder Mom was always cleaning.*

Easter is one of my favorite holidays. When I was a kid, we'd go to Mama Brown's house to celebrate. She'd hide hundreds of colorful plastic eggs all over her giant yard for me, Adam, and our cousins. It was such an ingrained tradition that even into adulthood we found ourselves at her house expecting the egg hunt. Mama Brown was a good sport, and I think we were all well into our 20's when she finally passed the baton and asked that Easter take place somewhere else.

I decided to host Easter at my house and was excited to start a new tradition. Dean and I were busy in the kitchen cooking when Dad and Mama Brown showed up. They were an hour early, but I had come to completely expect that from Dad.

"How about some coffee Dad?

"Ya, that sounds good!"

Dad grabbed one of the hard-boiled eggs I had dyed and put out for decoration. He banged the egg on the table and began removing its shell, leaving it strewn all over the fancy runner I had carefully put out.

"Have you got a plate and some salt and pepper?"

"Sure Dad" I said, as I maneuvered around him cleaning the mess he had managed to create before any of the other guests had even arrived.

Dad was unpredictable, but this was a routine I could count on. I always started preparing the food far in advance to make sure something was ready to eat when he showed up early. Sometimes, Dad would come two hours in advance. The bottom line was he came when he wanted to and then managed to stuff himself with food and drink before any of the other guests arrived. After that, he'd groan in satisfaction and flop on the couch to take a nap.

The condition of Dad's clothing was a stark representation of how he chose to live. He wore life proudly, right on his shirt: coffee stains, food, cigarette holes, and whatever else came his way. Everything he owned was destroyed. That's probably why he loved getting new clothes for his birthday or Christmas. Watching him open any gift was an experience. He'd fiercely attack the paper, tearing through it in seconds. He'd usually grunt a bit, like it was taking a big effort. Then, if any type of new clothing was in the box, he would immediately bring the garment right up to his nose, take a big sniff, and holler with approval. *Dad's nose really did seem to navigate much of his life.* If he really liked what you got him, he'd strip his clothes off right there in the middle of the party, so he could put on his new duds. We knew enough by then to get him a robe- he could put that on right over his clothes.

When Dad wasn't spilling life all over himself, he was dropping his lit cigarettes. He talked so fast and flailed his arms with such animation that holding a cigarette proved nearly impossible. Who knows, maybe he dropped his cigarettes on purpose just to entertain you with the hollering retrieval dance. Sometimes he'd snatch his cigarette up after dropping it and shove the thing back in his mouth backwards, with the lit end inside his mouth.

Dad knew he was not allowed to smoke inside my house but would always test the limits and light up in the living room. I'd chase him out yelling, and he'd scurry out onto the balcony with a wicked grin on his face. He'd sit on my balcony most of the time chain-smoking, and if my kids went out to keep him company, he'd offer them one of his cigarettes. I had to keep a close vigil. I hovered like a helicopter guarding over my kids, knowing full well Dad would corrupt them without hesitation.

Dad couldn't even extinguish a cigarette in a conventional manner. I always placed an ashtray outside for him, but he'd flick the cherry off and then use his thumb and finger to squeeze the life from his cigarette. Then he'd put the half-smoked thing back into the box to finish later. When he did attempt to use the ashtray, he would never tamp his cigarette out completely and it would lie there still smoking, stinking. I was amazed that he had managed to start only two small fires while living with Grandma. Luckily, Grandma was home to help extinguish the larger of the two. It raged up the outside stucco wall and cracked the large windowpane before she could douse it with water.

Dad's showing up early was almost as likely as him coming to a family celebration *high*. I came to expect this disappointment. There is not a Christmas in memory when Dad was sober. I came to tolerate his behavior because I felt I didn't have much choice. But when Dad brought cocaine to my Easter celebration and snorted lines in my bathroom, I thought I would kill him. He had never been that brazen; he had always used his drugs prior to arriving to a family celebration.

I didn't find out what Dad had done until the party ended. I was furious. I called him on the telephone and confronted him. "Don't you ever bring drugs into my home or around my kids again! Don't you know what I do for a fucking living? I lock people like you up. Why are you putting me in this position?" I yelled. Dad admitted to using drugs in my bathroom, but he did not care about my feelings. "I'm not on probation to you." He said defiantly. Dad was more pissed than I was and demanded to know which family member had tattled and betrayed him. This absurd question hurt even more. Shortly after that, I received a letter from Dad.

Hi Amber, Glad the party broke up early without any more tension for me. Brings back a lot of history. Past that negates life's pleasantries; they are downers to ME NOW! I have NO reason to carry those any more. It was nice to see Eddie and the food was good. I apologize for NOT respecting your house rules. But you must also respect my choices for all my decisions, including Drugs or any other direction I'm heading in... I am a responsible Grandpa with a lot of input to my decisions and you are crowding my style. Accept this choice and resolve IT AS IS—end of conversation Darlin. Your concerns are well documented and understood as they were intended. But not acceptable for Me. Please re-think our history together. It has always been mutually supporting in all areas! No? "Needs" are being met; satisfaction is resulting from usage. The "laws" are wrong as *usual. Your whole life is ahead of you. A lot will happen, and you will overcome many obstacles and be responsible for many others in times ahead of you. Thus, you will also be entitled to 100% of your actions regardless of laws or rules of society. Let's start NOW; redefine your bad thoughts or worries when we cross this path again. Some day you will understand anyway. Try to get a grip ahead of time. I love you very much and I respect and admire you. But you are wrong to judge me on this one and I will pull rank on you and be angered and hurt that you forced me to put a fence between us. If it wasn't important, I would not put it in this fashion. If I was wrong, I'd already know it and still do it. But I'm NOT Amber. I've earned the right to be a proud man of good heart and mind. You are my blood and heart daughter who is closer to me than any other living soul on Earth. Look back on your own path's direction. It's far more interesting than mine and a lot of decisions are coming your way that you will carry for a long time to come. I'll be there supporting each decision. Love ya, Dad.*

CHAPTER 20

How can something that feels this good be bad?

When Dad moved to Mama Brown's house, he was able to do some handy-work around the house, but he had no idea how to repair the crummy old plumbing. Mama Brown hated paying for things she could fix herself, but plumbing was definitely beyond her scope. The money she shelled out on plumbing repairs vexed her, and she told Dad, "If I ever decided to get hitched again, I'd go find myself a plumber to marry!" Dad decided right then that he would become a plumber. He found a job apprenticing, learned the trade, got licensed, and had Mama Brown finance his next business venture: his own plumbing business.

Dad got laid off from his high-paying aerospace job a number of times in the 1990's, but in 1999 things came to a permanent end. Dad had run out of money and had finally accepted the fact that he would not be called back to work. Mama Brown had been living on the hill by herself since Grandpa died a couple of years earlier, and it was agreed that Dad would return home to live with her. I'm not sure whether either party thought the arrangement was temporary.

I thought the living situation would be good for Dad. Finally, he would be accountable to someone. Grandma certainly wasn't going to allow him to do drugs and misbehave. I was wrong. Over the years they had their fights about the household rules and Grandma's expectations, but strangely, Dad always seemed to prevail, even though Grandma held all the cards.

Dad moved out once to protest Grandma's rules. He rented a room down the street from her house, but that arrangement didn't last long. Strangers were less willing to put up with Dad's bullshit, and after he threatened to "get froggy" with his new roommate, his occupancy was terminated. He went back to Grandma's house humbled and gracious, but his thankful attitude was short-lived, and he quickly took back complete control of Grandma and her house.

As Grandma aged, her ability and willingness to hold Dad to any type of standard dwindled. Initially, she had an attitude of no tolerance regarding his drug use and would not allow drugs in her home. But Dad whittled away at Grandma and she became exhausted by his behavior. Eventually, she succumbed to his *will* and gave up any hope of controlling him.

A couple of years after Dad moved in with Grandma he was diagnosed with emphysema. He totally exploited his illness and constantly told Grandma, "Mama, just take care of me one more day. I'm dying...I may be dead tomorrow." He said this in dramatic jest, and it was a private joke they shared. Once Dad had his diagnosis, his drug habit seemed to escalate. I know he figured... *What the hell, I'm dying anyway.*

Over the span of about ten years, Dad was able to utterly brainwash Grandma. She was under his spell, just as Mom had been years ago. Grandma went from an attitude of "no tolerance" with Dad's drug use to financing his habit. Once, she told me, "You know, I have to have cash available; sometimes he wakes up really desperate." Grandma's behavior confused and angered me. Dad made no effort to hide his drug use. He always believed that his honesty should totally excuse his behavior, and he expected his family to accept and support his choices no matter how destructive they were.

Grandma bought into this ridiculous ideology and Dad's behavior worsened. Eventually, he was able to snort cocaine right there in the television room. I will never know how he was able to completely destroy Grandma's set of virtuous principles, but he succeeded. Grandma was liberated from her ethical compass and began to live by Dad's mantra, "*How can something that feels this good be bad?*" Her behavior began to mirror Dad's, and she took to cussing. Her new motto was "Fuck it!" She said it with gusto and she meant it.

I was at work sitting at my desk when suddenly, I was overtaken with grief. The little radio on my desk was playing Sara McLaughlin's song "Angel," and I began to sob. I pictured Dad dead, *in the arms of an angel.* Dad was killing himself. Why did I stand idly by? I had spent the past eight years counseling and aiding addicts in their recovery. I talked to hundreds of kids about the dangers of drug use, the perils of gang involvement, and the importance of family and making wise choices. Why did I try so hard with strangers and put no effort into Dad? Had I given up on him entirely?

I decided to write Dad a letter. I wanted to tell him how much I loved him. How much I wished he could live a drug-free life. I mailed off my letter with a copy of the song "Angel." Maybe the music would move him as it had moved me. A couple of days later I received a response.

6/3/2005

Hi Ambie,

I listened to "In the Arms of an Angel" several times this morning. I played it again. This is truly a beautiful song. The message is clear and the presentation is smooth, just like you darling. I get a lot of comfort from my part in your contributions to this beautiful world. You are my ultimate pleasure and world class treasure. Changing my life style is not the easiest thing in the world to do, but with the help of a message like this one (song) it is certainly a help and inspiration.

Love ya, Papa D.

Maybe hope was not lost....

CHAPTER 21

Ruminations of a mad man

2009 was a bad year. Dad's health was failing. When he came for Easter he labored so hard to breathe that we thought we'd lose him right there, smoking cigarettes on the balcony. His drug habit seemed to worsen. He hated feeling so helpless. W*e hated it too*. We all thought Dad was going to die, and his journal proved that he felt the same way.

Saturday, January 24th 2009 3:30 am

Life is comfortable in these final stages of emphysema, lack of air days of mine. I would rather document clear evidence of my understanding of these last few days.

I'm not depressed about this crap and I don't allow for any damn spoilage during my days or nights. I use only the very best of everything I consume: restaurants, fast food, fuel, drugs, parts, supplies.

Spoiled? You bet I am and won't settle for anything less. As long as Mama Brown is alive and well enough to cater to all my demands, I am perfectly happy and satisfied. I am confident in all my achievements and there were plenty of them too. I am at peace with my Lord.

All my electronics work and new batteries are plentiful around here at the castle in the sky. We are stocked up like a restaurant and most of the old plumbing has been repaired. Plumbing is a very nice passion to be able to lean on and I do, heavily.

I seek out the edges to protect my balancing skills…if you don't live as I have you are clearly taking up too much space. I am a consumer of life, not a collector of worthless circles. I spend money freely on everything that keeps me warm and fuzzy. I choose pretty carefully each task that I want to perform.

Many of our "laws" interfere with our needs and should be disregarded. I don't hurt anybody and defy thoughtless suggestions to the contrary. I feel like an insider, so I must be one. I am pleased with my son Adam and Debra and their two boys, my grandsons AJ and Brandon. I am pleased with my daughter Amber, Dean, and their two boys, Conner and Carson, and the puppy too, damn it.

My "tracks" aren't that hard to follow. I usually document my behavior patterns regardless of their incriminating nature. Early morning "writing" has always been one of my favorite things to do. Most of my letters have been sent to my good friends Ken and Anne, who have been instructed to read and burn some of the more revealing things I've done or said over the last 30 years. This special letter is designed for my family and closest friends, as few as I might have. It's hard to get into my inner circle—by design.

If you've put your shit together properly, it will set you free. That will do as my best contribution to my best people.

I have fired up a fresh new smoke while sucking in cool compressed oxygen in the van while driving down the highway a dozen times…an explosive way out for some…not on my list of needs.

I'm picking up a nebulizer at Amber's house this morning. Why didn't my doctor advise me of this possibility? You can bet your ass I'm going to ask her what else she isn't telling me about curing my way out….

February 4th 2009

Every move costs you energy and oxygen that you don't have anymore. You get pretty tired of that shit real quick. Don't argue about the drug shit, you'll still lose. I take what eases the pain. I'd drink gasoline if it worked for me.

A half ounce a week for you slow learners; 1/16 of an ounce a day is a good quantity for my needs: to work, drive, collect helpers, and anything else I do is not interfered with but made possible by what's left of my wonderful body.

I'm not mad. I'm on easy street for a change. I know I've been putting a big anchor on Mama's head and body strength, but she minds me so well. Any man would be spoiled by mom's pleasures. Reality is for all those people who can't handle drugs properly.

For the last three months, check out time and end of program is on my mind. Death can only get sweeter when you flirt closer to her...it's a "she." I'm okay with the "Powers that be" and have no pressing needs to fulfill. That's a good feeling.

I make a lot of "noise" fighting to live. I haven't given up the fight, but when I do, I will be at PEACE. Weight loss. Can't eat and breathe at the same time with any comfort. Exhausting consumption of air comes with any movement, especially in the walking mode. Sitting quietly is a rewarded function. Liquid food goes down with more ease but also comes up frequently. Wonderful existence huh? It's okay, I'm not mad. You'd have to be a fool not to see a final act encroaching to ease the fight. Yep! And it's okay.

February 5th, 2009 6:00 am

My personal "Hot" items:

1. *Viva paper towels*

2. *A wonderful, accomplished business to draw from and sell if I can*

3. *Feeling "Rich" up here with Mama Brown. I enjoy using her to spoil every need I come up with and she does very well*

4. *Smoking good weed relaxes me just fine*

5. *Plenty of Juice (cocaine) to set "Me free"-- reality is for those who can't handle drugs.*

6. *Free to choose my every thought; yep! Think about that one for a moment*

7. *No fucking bills to pay.*

8. *Plenty of fuel: smokes, Juice, yep those are what's left of my sweet pleasures.*

9. *Nothing tastes better than sweet oxygen, but the lungs don't always accommodate the air and that's okay too!*

10. *Nebulizer was a sweet addition Ambie! Thanks.*

To all~ go forth and hope that you can feel this fucking good when it's your turn to sleep.

February 21, 2009

Savor your individual chemistry cause it's real. Those things you ingest that feel so right would kill another person but that's only cause they don't listen to their body's clear signal, and we all get them. Hi Am, Hi Joyce, Hi Mom, Hi Conner, Hi Carson. Nicotine, caffeine, cocaine, albuterol, and fish tacos work very well in my body. But don't you try my combo....

August 7, 2009

Question...what drugs do for me. Emotional stress, physical pain, innermost deepest feelings of inferiority, fears, pitiful feelings, every wrong thing you ever did in your younger life, forgiven. Removed simultaneously from your mind and soul, your stomach, legs, arms, head, feet, and hands are caressed in the arms of six angels or seventy-seven virgins, or whatever you see as your savior in heaven or hell or anywhere else. Do that for about 35 full seconds and you won't need any more.

CHAPTER 22

"You know, I did the best I could with him"

"I punched him right in his big fucking nose." Dad bragged. I cringed and was suddenly grateful I couldn't make it to the family gathering to witness the event firsthand. Apparently, Dad was insulted by his elderly uncle. A sweet man who I suspect did not deserve the humiliation of being punched and wrestled to the ground. Dad was indignant, happy with his decision, and seemed to suffer no consequences. That was the last time my uncle came to any family celebration.

2009

Dad called me at work that November and said Mama Brown was in route to the hospital. She had fallen off a ladder while putting up Christmas lights. The woman was 85 years old and had no business on a ladder but arguing with her was pointless. The family protested the year before when she spent weeks on a ladder painting the exterior trim of her house. Grandma scoffed and told us "There's no way I'm going to pay for something I can do myself."

The hospital was right next door to my workplace, so I immediately responded. I was ushered into the emergency area and saw Grandma laying there on a gurney. Her hair was soaked with blood and her earlobe was torn. I immediately began to cry. The most active, healthy senior on the planet…taken down by her own damn ladder. It wasn't supposed to happen this way. Grandma seemed out of it and moaned in pain. The doctors told me that she suffered a brain bleed, two broken ribs, a fractured vertebra, and lacerations. "My god is she going to live?" I yelled. They reassured me the only real threat was the brain bleed, and they intended to monitor this closely.

Mama Brown spent the following weeks at the hospital and in a convalescent home. I visited frequently to ensure that the doctors and nurses knew someone was watching. I questioned the medication they prescribed, the roommate she was given, and the food she was delivered. I lodged a complaint with one facility and made regular phone calls to the physician. No one was going to mess with Grandma on my watch.

Mom and I were at the convalescent hospital visiting Grandma one morning when Dad showed up. Grandma had almost fully recovered but did not want to return home for some reason. I'm pretty sure I knew why.

Dad came into the room out of breath and completely *high*. The muscles in his face contorted and he made grunting noises as he gasped for air. His drug habit kept him looking thin, but his emphysema had further robbed him of his health. He literally could not breathe. Dad sat down in the chair, but his legs continued to move and bounce around. He looked really bad, skinnier and dirtier than usual, with cuts and lesions on his hands and arms.

Dad coughed, hacked, and gasped for air as he told us a story. "By the time I got in here from the parking lot, I had run out of breath. I sat down in the hallway to rest, and one of the nurses offered to help me to my room. She thought I lived here!" Dad thought this was hilarious and laughed until he spit up in a napkin. I felt grateful that he actually *had* a napkin. Many times, he would spit phlegm right into the palm of his hand then flick the mucus into a trash can or right on the floor. I never got used to the revolting sound of Dad's cough. The deep gurgling sound could never be cleared by his hacking. You could literally hear him drowning in his own mucus. Every breath was a struggle.

Dad's restless visit lasted a mere five minutes. There was a long silence after his departure. I think each of us contemplated addressing "the elephant in the room." The silence was broken with laughter after Grandma said, "You know, I did the best I could with him." Mom and I finished up our visit with Grandma and reassured her we would stop by the house to check on Dad. He had been completely unsupervised since her accident weeks earlier. With no one to clean up after Dad, I knew the house would be a mess, but I was not prepared for what I saw. The house was filthy, and Dad had obviously been smoking cigarettes inside, something Grandma had not permitted. The kitchen table was covered with cigarette butts, trash, and about twenty tablets of paper he'd scrawled on. Dad's handwriting was very distinctive, like that of a doctor's: barely legible. He didn't use one tablet of paper to write down his thoughts. Each new thought required a new tablet of paper, a way to organize his scattered thoughts; the *ruminations of a mad man.*

I was bowled over. I had seen this type of chaos and disarray when I had gone to conduct home calls of people on probation. The fact that Dad was living in this type of squalor drew a sharp parallel. He was not unlike the drug addicts I dealt with at work, and this realization left me feeling nauseated.

Dad moved at a frantic pace and immediately put us to work. He wanted his sheets and laundry washed. He wanted the dishes done, and he wanted the trash taken out. Dad had me take an old television, clothes, and a number of photo albums out to the dumpster. "Dad, why are you throwing these photos away?" I asked as I flipped through one of the books. I caught a glimpse of the Hawaii trip Dad took Adam on years earlier, the vacation I had not been included in. I instantly felt a pang of hurt and anger but quickly remembered why it was better I hadn't gone: Dad decided to hire a prostitute for Adam while there. He was pretty impressed when Adam turned down the offer and told Dad, "I want my first time to be special."

Dad was desperate to rid himself of his property and his memories. It scared me and made me suspicious. Why did he want to obliterate memories captured in the photo albums? What was he trying to hide? Then I thought the horrible thought…. *Did Grandma really fall off the ladder or was it kicked out from beneath her?* I felt guilty even thinking something so terrible, but indeed, Dad was killing Grandma slowly…what was the difference?

Mom and I finished Dad's chores dutifully, and as we were saying goodbye, Dad insisted that he give me Christmas money from Grandma.

I told Dad that I didn't think it was appropriate for him to be doling out Grandma's money. "Dad, don't worry about that. If Grandma wants to send Christmas money, then she will…." "Well, if you don't want to take it, I'll give your share to Adam." Dad often kept things competitive between Adam and I. He knew I always felt second best, and he confirmed the legitimacy of my fears more than once. *Dad admitted that the disparity I felt was real, not imagined.*

I took the money and wrote Grandma a thank you letter explaining that Dad had given me money *from her*. You can imagine how awful this felt when I learned that Dad had relieved Grandma of $15,000.00 during her hospital stay. He telephoned me just to brag about what he'd done. I never knew what motivated Dad to *tell on himself*. I don't know if he was attempting to share guilt by making me privy to the information, or if he wanted to confess his sins and rid himself of the guilt. Sometimes I think he was proud of his dastardly deeds.

Dad's flagrance was astounding. He told me that the bank caught on to Grandma's dwindling account, and they froze all transactions. Dad marched right in to the bank and demanded they reinstate his ability to draw funds. His name was listed on the account. How dare they presume to shut off access to *his* money? The bank acquiesced, and Dad continued to draw money from the account. When Grandma came home from the hospital and learned Dad had pillaged her account, she confronted him but this accomplished little. He made no apology for his actions. He felt entitled to the money. He justified his behavior and turned reason on its head just as he always did. Grandma went away feeling guilty. *How dare she go and injure herself leaving him alone in his weakened state. After all, he was dying of emphysema!*

CHAPTER 23

Death Protest

D ad's behavior was totally abnormal. I didn't understand it but really wanted to. Once I asked him why he wanted to destroy himself. "What's wrong Dad? I sense you are tortured inside. Did something happen to you in the past? Did someone hurt you?" Dad said "No," but I will always wonder if there was a truth even he wasn't willing to reveal.

"I've got a surprise for you," Dad said. "Really, what is it?" I asked. "You have to come and get it. It's amazing." "I'm intrigued," I said. Dad had never surprised me with anything before. I knew he could never keep it a surprise. "Well, give me a hint" I prodded. "It's millions of years old." "Wow…then it must be a rock or fossil of some sort." "It's no rock…it's *a stone* with a thousand crystals in it!" "A geode?" I asked. "A what?" "A geode…you know one of those rocks they break open and find gems inside." "Yes, exactly!" Dad said. "Wow Dad! Sounds amazing, I can't wait to see it!" "Well come over and get it, but bring Dean, it's a heavy fucker." "Geez Dad, how big is it? Do I need a crane?" Dad laughed. "Maybe, it's three or four feet tall." "My God, where did you get it?" "I was at a friend's house and saw the thing in his garage. I have never seen anything like it before, I was nuts about it. My buddy was hard up for cash and so I offered to buy it from him…you know, with my allowance."

Dad had been receiving ten thousand dollars a year from grandma since I could remember; It was some type of tax write-off for her. He spent the money frivolously and wantonly. It was always gone in two months without even a thought for his kids or grandkids. The fact that Dad had actually thought of buying something for me with the money surprised me.

"Gosh Dad, I'm flattered you thought of me when you had that wad of cash in your pocket." "Well, to tell you the truth, I didn't. I just had to have those stones. I bought two of them. I'm going to give Grandma the other one." How nice Dad. I can't wait to see it." I said, disappointed.

Dean and I drove out two days later to see Dad and pick up the geode. A geologist was at the house to authenticate and appraise the geode. Dad sat there beaming as the man explained the intricacies of the stone. It was a deep purple amethyst that sparkled beautifully in the sunlight. I was moved by Dad's semi-selfless act. I couldn't remember any other time that he had given to me quite like this, without obligation of a holiday or birthday. I no longer cared that he purchased the stone without giving a thought to who he would give it to...*he decided to give it to me.*

January 2011

Aunt Arline died shortly after Christmas. I saw her weeks earlier, when the family gathered at our house to celebrate the holiday. Auntie had made every member of the family a loaf of her famous zucchini bread, just as she had done every past year I could remember. She always found a quiet moment during the party to hand deliver her homemade bread with a knowing smile; *my loaf still sat in the freezer.* She had lived to a ripe-old 90 years, but her black hair and pretty skin suggested many more Christmases I wish I had hugged her more tightly when she left my house that night.

The funeral took place at Rose Hills, where my sweet Grandpa Brown was buried. Auntie was a relative on Mom's side of the family, but I knew Dad would be there. He never missed a funeral. He was deeply sensitive despite his abrasive exterior. I also think he was fascinated by the morbidity of death, an old friend he had successfully been able to elude the better half of his life. Unfortunately, Christmas and funerals were two of Dad's favorite occasions on which to "self-medicate." I knew that in all probability he would attend the funeral *"high as a kite."*

I made Auntie a beautiful flower arrangement with yellow and pink roses; she was such a soft, gentle soul. I didn't want the kids to experience a funeral at their young age, so Dean and I dropped them off at school and headed to Rose Hills for the graveside service. When we arrived, I saw Dad's plumbing van parked near the gravesite and wondered where Grandma was. She usually drove Dad in her car. Clearly, they had driven there separately. Alarmed, I approached the grieving mob and immediately saw Dad lying in the grass near the casket. There were only three rows of seats, which were already occupied by Auntie's elderly Mason buddies. It was standing room only. Dad was clearly exhausted by the journey and was without a seat.

I said hello to a few relatives, then made a bee-line for Dad to assess the need for "damage control." *It was entirely acceptable for me to "talk shit" on Dad, but by God, nobody else better!* As I got closer, I could see his chest heaving. He labored so hard to take in air; I suspect some people thought we might need to dig another grave. Dad sat perched to the side, propped up by one arm, with his legs in a fetal tuck. For the first time, he looked weak and vulnerable. It was hard for me to watch, but it didn't seem to bother the old biddies sitting in chairs; none of them offered up their seats.

Dad's emphysema had consumed his body and his arrogance. His once exuberant charisma had vanished. I gave Dad a hug and said hello to Adam, who was already standing guard over Dad. Then I took a double take of Dad's jacket, which had white powder strewn all over its upper half. I looked around furtively and began dusting him off. "Dad, what's all over you, 'Baby Powder'?" I said dumbly. I looked back at Dean; his eyes were bulging, and he was biting his lip trying not to laugh. Mama Brown then looked at Dad's jacket and said, "I don't know what that is!"

The funeral began, and Dad lay there in the grass the entire time. As inappropriate as he looked sprawled out on the lawn near the casket, I couldn't help but feel thankful that his "death protest" was a peaceful demonstration rather than an angry revolt. I couldn't help wondering if he was lying there pondering his own mortality…challenging death. Dad's mortality was certainly on the forefront of my mind. I couldn't stop thinking of the eulogy I would inevitably give for him…or the ones I had written over the years as a child.

Suddenly, I felt very grateful that we had decided not to bring our boys to the funeral. Over the years, Conner and Carson came to discover Papa Dean's shortcomings. He certainly was not your typical grandfather. He was not permitted to spend any time with the boys unless directly supervised and for that reason they remained shielded from the magnitude of the situation. Dad was never made aware of my rule. It didn't much matter though, he did not appear to desire much time with his grandsons anyway. Conner and Carson loved their Papa Dean, but knew he was a drug addict. This fact was not hidden from them and Papa Dean was often used as an example- of what *not* to do.

After the funeral, we visited with some relatives and then got into the car to meet some family members at the Mason Lodge. As we pulled away from the gravesite, I saw Mama Brown kneeling down over my Grandpa's headstone. She busied herself picking weeds and arranging the artificial flowers placed there long ago. "Stop the car Dean!" I yelled. I got out of the car and gave Grandma a long hug. I knew she went to visit Grandpa's grave frequently, but I hadn't been there since the funeral nearly fifteen years ago. I was overcome with a sadness knowing that she would have to bury Dad too. Even in times of despair, her strength was staggering. She had just attended auntie's funeral and glimpsed an eerie premonition of Dad's fate. Yet, still, she smiled and hummed a little tune as she primped Grandpa's headstone.

I got back into the car and we drove away from Rose Hills. After a long silence Dean said with a smile, "So, what the hell was all over your Dad's jacket?" We both spontaneously broke into laughter pondering the absurdity of the situation…Dad lying there next to the casket barely able to breathe with cocaine strewn all over his stained dinner jacket. Dean speculated that Dad pulled a "Scarface" before the funeral and stuck his whole face in a pile of cocaine. We laughed ourselves silly and decided this was the only plausible scenario to explain the powdery white explosion. Indeed, it was no laughing matter, but laughter was much easier than the alternative.

In April, things took a turn for the worse. Dad called me excited and agitated and said that he had just gotten into a major fight with Grandma. Dad was smoking in the house again, and when Grandma confronted him and told him to go outside to smoke, he flicked his lit cigarette at her. Grandma saw red and punched Dad right in the face. I was shocked. Had Grandma reached her breaking point? Was she finally going to forbid Dad's terrible behavior and tell him to shape up or ship out?

Dad said that Grandma thought it would be a good idea if he went to Adam's house so they could have time to "cool off." Once Mom caught wind that Dad planned to spend a week or two with Adam's family, she flew off the handle and telephoned Dad to give him a piece of her mind. Mom knew Dad used drugs. She deemed him a horrible role model, and she did not want him around her grandkids. Dad was outraged that Mom dared interfere. He felt it was none of her business and he said he would never forgive her.

While Dad was at Adam's house, I telephoned Grandma to see how she was getting along. Grandma was exhausted and upset. She told me Dad recently took her credit card and stole $4000.00. He slid her card right through the credit card terminal Grandma bought him to use for his plumbing business. When she confronted him; he was indignant. She told him that she would hide her credit cards in the future, to which he responded, "Go ahead, I already have the numbers." Grandma did not know what to do about Dad and felt powerless. I spent the next hour on the phone counseling her. I told her to stop enabling Dad. She seemed to take the advice to heart and obviously had a conversation with him when he returned, because I promptly received a letter from him detailing his contempt for what I had done. I had tattled on him and empowered Grandma, and he was beyond angry.

4/16/2011

Hi Amber,

I love you Am and always will. I've made it a point not to interfere in anyone's life and/or decisions, yet I'm comfortable in opining anything if asked to.

Your decision to route Mama Brown into an "enabler" position with respects to my Juice intake was a bold move with all good intentions but has clearly backfired in your lap.

I'm disappointed with your choice and will not tolerate any further attempts to make any corrections with respect to my choices.

Mother and I have a good healthy relationship with each other and don't lie to one another. She was kind enough to share your conversation with her, and I thanked her for doing so. As a result, neither of us were comfortable with your accusations or suggestions to change our current actions or behavioral patterns, right or wrong. I want you to be aware of all feelings and results of conversations as you should be.

I'm 65, semi-retired, and never been arrested or spent one minute in jail. I have never been convicted of any crime. I am completely responsible for all my actions and choices. I've raised my family and feel very comfortable with the results of my actions, decisions, and family welfare.

I'm asking you to respect my choices and lifestyle. I won't overlap into your family's health or business no matter how small the interference. I won't allow outside influences that judge my happiness or comfort zones.

My stay with Adam and family went very well from Sat. 9th of April to Sat. 16th of April despite your mother's wishes for me not to go. She was wrong and unacceptable and severed any possibility of bonding between her and me. I'll never forgive or forget her unjustifiable intrusion in my wishes to bond with Adam's family, and I certainly did.

I was asked by Debra to come back and stay another week with both dogs when they go on vacation with their new boat and I will be there for that purpose.

Know that any choices you make now, and in the future will be fine with me as they always have been in the past. However, all decisions carry repercussions should they be inconsistent or interfere with purpose. There is nothing I can't correct from my side of the fence and I'm far beyond the attempts by others to persuade alternative patterns that bring them comfort; don't make that error in judgment about my personal choices, as they are clearly mine to make, live with, and pay for in every respect; do you agree? And I will fight for your right to stand by all your decisions past, present, and future.

Cancel my visit this Easter, nor does Mama Brown want to come. This came entirely from her, not at my suggestion. Her driving is not good for me, but the full reason for my non-compliance visit was 100% in response to your conversation with her with 100% respect to your enabler *remarks.*

Your decisions not to allow drug influences in your family are completely understood and 100% agreed with, but my decision to partake has nothing to do with your family's safety or contact with my drug intake- 10-4?

Accept it or don't. This is clearly your choice and I'm OK with all your decisions. I've been as honest and forthcoming as I can and I will never withhold a lie from you. Your judgments will always be fine with me and so are Mine. *Life isn't that complicated, and it has certainly been a full pleasure to me in all respects.*

Mother and I have a great working relationship and my life has been much better because I've been able to stay here and enjoy every damned day. Her life has not been negatively affected by my Juice nor should she be made to feel guilty for allowing me to live as I choose.

She doesn't deserve that kind of pressure from you or anyone else… are you with me? I'm not a misbehaving adolescent experimenting with drugs, take another look and be comfortable with all your choices. I am!

Love ya,

Papa Dean

After reading the letter I wasn't sure whether I was more angry or sad. This *asshole* really was the most selfish man on earth. The way he was able to completely justify his needs and believe he was not affecting others in the process was outrageous! I cried and then promptly sat down to draft a retort.

4/17/2011

I love you too Pops and always will. You have raised me to be a no-nonsense, dreadfully honest person. So, I'm sorry you don't like my opinion; I just call em' how I see em.'

You say that you have made it a point to "not interfere in anyone's life and or decisions," which is partially true. You have always been supportive of my choices, and I have always respected and appreciated this confidence you offered. However, when you say you don't interfere in others' lives you do not consider the impact you have had on us all. Your behavior directly affects those around you, and you have trouble acknowledging that fact.

I have had a very unconventional upbringing with an alcoholic mother and a drug addict father. You seem to give little thought with regard to how difficult this dysfunction has been for me to process both cognitively and emotionally, let alone overcome and be satisfied with.

Most of the time I feel resigned to what cannot be changed; other times, I feel fucking cheated! Cheated from a normal childhood experience, cheated from what my friends enjoyed, cheated from an innocence I don't think I ever enjoyed.

Not to say that my submersion into the real shitty-ness of life was all negative. I am a stronger person for it. That doesn't mean I'm not resentful sometimes or angry.

I don't know if you have ever really contemplated my life experience, especially as it relates to the stark contrast it resembles to yours. You had normal and very supportive parents who spoiled you rotten... and still do. They acted in a parental role. Anyway, I ramble...I just don't think you understand the impact your behavior had on me then or now with your serious and sometimes detrimental "interference."

So, forgive me if you feel as though I am trying to "correct" you or "tattle" on you; that is not my intention. I know any hope of you changing is absurd, but you choose not to see some basic truths and you become angry when they are pointed out. You told me that you steal money from grandma. That is not what I consider a "healthy relationship."

You taught me not to be a thief and I would never steal from you or any other family member. You also told me what happened the day you and Grandma got into a fight, and this too makes me very sad. I love you and Grandma both and I want you to take care of one another, not assault one another. That is not what I consider "healthy." I don't consider my conversation with Grandma as inappropriate. She was upset and expressed concern with regard to some of your behaviors, as they were having a negative impact on her spirit and happiness. I offered some encouragement and advice as to maintaining healthy boundaries so that your behavior would not "interfere" with how she wants to live. I'm not attempting to control or correct your behavior only Grandma can choose to do that. I don't perceive my conversation with Grandma as "backfiring" on me either. I see this as an opportunity to have meaningful communication. You seem to think I'm judging your happiness also; I am not. Your happiness is clear, yet I don't know if you always consider the happiness of those around you.

We have always enjoyed a very honest relationship with one another and I don't intend to change that now. I will always communicate my feelings to you and will not sugar coat shit or tell you lies. I'm sorry if you do not like the truth or my truth anyway.

To say that Grandma isn't negatively impacted by your "Juice" is untrue. Everyone is affected by it, mostly me and Adam. I was impacted when I got to see you shaking in a hospital bed after you OD'ed two different fucking times. You think that doesn't stick with a kid? I got to watch you give cocaine to my brother and then condemn me for being a hypocrite. You think that stuff was easy to shake off as a teenager?

Even in my adult life I am impacted and really long for a relationship with you in which drugs are not more important than me. I have accepted the sad truth. I lost you to drugs and trust me, the notion that you believe I am trying to change you is laughable. I stopped trying to do that a LONG time ago.

If Grandma is feeling guilt it is not because I made her feel that way and you are right, nobody should be pressuring her. Not me, you, or anyone else. Grandma is a tough nut and can take care of herself. Live how you'd like, you always have. But don't underestimate or fail to acknowledge how this impacts others because trust me…it does.

I know that dying sucks and I know that you feel frustrated by the process that is occurring to your body and spirit, but I will not let you off the hook when I've got something to say. Your dying will not act as an excuse to not "keep it real" and call you out. But I would rather be on loving terms when you depart this earth. I will accept your choices as I have no other choice. Just as I have ALWAYS done. If you feel your absence at Easter will adequately "punish" me, so be it. I will set a place for you and you are still welcome should you change your mind.

Love ya too, A

Two days later, I received another letter from Dad.

Parenting is a difficult and long process as you would surely agree....
We all do the best we can at the time and make corrections as we
learn better ways to raise our young. No? The bottom line remains
the same. How do the children end up as adults in a very difficult
world around us?

Both my children are degreed and own their own homes. Both have
highly respected careers. Both are married and both have two beau-
tiful boys of their own to raise.

If you are fortunate enough to be able to see these powerful accom-
plishments from your two boys (both of them), then you too will
have been as successful as I have in raising mine. Did I make a few
mistakes along the way? Was I a dysfunctional father who took ille-
gal drugs as a choice? Did I lie about taking the drugs? I not only
accept the truth, I make damn sure that you are completely aware of
all my behavior without exception, and if you interpret that as losing
your innocence or being cheated out of a "normal" upbringing, then
it is a fair trade off...don't you think?

Ecstasy at night clubs, excessive drinking: Oh well. How bad can that
really be? Does it negatively affect the rest of your life? Are drugs, any
drugs really more important than your blood children? Think about
that statement very carefully for a moment.

No matter how you accomplish your goals in life, the bottom line is:
How well did your two boys turn out as productive adults?

Did Adam really tell you that he has been negatively affected by My Behavior patterns as your note of 4/16/2011 asserts? That's not the same message that he shares with me about our relationships—past present and future....

I'm sure that both your boys will be proud and productive adults. No less than both of mine have...and we sure did choose different techniques to make our kids adapt and overcome!

This note has been well thought out and completely written while 100% under the influence of a controlled substance...100% Me darling, not the drugs talking here. Dysfunctional adult, drug addicted father? Is that how I'm read from anyone's point of view? That's their problem.

This is the best I can offer to anyone, and I'm pleased with the style with which I communicate these feelings to you, my very professional, highly productive, well-rounded, highly educated, beautiful daughter, mother, and wife.... Drugs more important than you? Lost me to drugs? Dysfunctional? Really? Look deeper!

"Triple Crown" adult children may be too high a goal for you to set for yourself with so many crucial decisions left for you to make ahead of you...so a less aggressive goal might be a safer option for you. It is a very competitive world out there, and many obstacles are ready to challenge all your attempts to succeed as well as I have.

I've kept and re-read your letter several times with complete understanding and agreement with all your feelings. The bottom line is the same. How did your children turn out? Yep, it takes a lot of work to do it right, and where is the manual on the correct process?

Mom and I will go to a nice Easter breakfast this morning at our local family diner. Yep, and get as fat as we can.

Love ya, Papa Dean—adapting and overcoming all obstacles.

Dad included three pages of notes from the letter I sent him. Basically, a list of 19 key points he took away from my letter. Most of the key points ended as a question…Drugs more important than you? You lost me to drugs? You think? You accept my choices? Really? At the end of the list he wrote in red, "Really feel that way from my behavior do ya? No shit." I wondered if my feelings were really a surprise to him. Then I second guessed myself and wondered if I was the crazy one. I called Adam to vent about Dad, hoping for some type of validation. Adam just listened. "Adam, am I fucking crazy? We were living with a mad man, right?" "Absolutely" he replied without hesitation.

I didn't write Dad back. The fact that he took ownership and responsibility for my success just pissed me off. I succeeded *despite of* him…not because of him. The lessons he taught were learned at a great cost and were often cruel. Yes, I had turned out alright, but I certainly wasn't ready to thank Dad for doing a bang-up job. Dad wanted me to believe that there was purpose behind his parenting methodology. That what *he* did produced highly adaptive, successful offspring. The way I saw it, *he just got real lucky*. Actually, Adam and I were lucky; Dad set us up for failure.

I didn't talk to Dad for two months. When Father's Day rolled around I got a pit in my stomach and briefly grappled with the option of *not* calling him. I couldn't bring myself to ignore Dad on Father's Day. I loved him and knew how sick he was; his time was limited. The conversation was short and sweet. "Hey Pops, happy Father's Day." "You better have called me," Dad said.

I kept a safe distance and spoke to Dad sporadically on the phone. When Christmas rolled around, I hadn't seen him for some time and wasn't quite prepared for his gaunt appearance. He came toting his oxygen tank like he normally did, but he looked far worse than usual. My dog wouldn't stop barking at him; I imagine he believed Dad was the walking dead. Dad's cheekbones protruded. Even the bones in his forehead seemed to jut out on the sides, defining his weight loss. I kissed Dad on the cheek, and a deep sadness settled over me. Dad had lost the twinkle in his eye. Being pissed off at someone who is dying is the ultimate conundrum. Peace and love prevail initially…then the hurt and anger come back for you when the dying is done.

CHAPTER 24

"Juice Talk"

Mom said she would love Dad till the day she died…the feeling was mutual. He'd love her till the day he died too.

December 30, 2011 Dad's Journal:

Juice talk-

Postage is going up in 2012 again, ain't it? Yep, and they are still losing money good old government; fail at a lot of stuff don't they? Damn the stamps I just bought—all say "forever' on them; should take care of the mail forever then, no?

I look unhealthily skinny because I am not consuming enough food to fill out the empty spaces between cells. I'll keep eating till it gets fixed to the proper fill levels in my body.

I'm still here, gang, fighting to stay with y'all. No wishes to depart tomorrow or even the next few months. Nope, not me. I'm a sick guy with lots of money to spend freely as I'd like, No?

You damn well know that I'll be buying a nice FAT bag of juice to quench my sweet tooth for spring time. Tingling between my blood cells, yep that too. 14 grams ain't that much…8 or 9 days of normal appetite. I've done it dozens of times before without any problems at all. Nope.

Even get it for half the cost of normal daily purchases and save all the gas and time to connect on a daily schedule. I just don't always have enough money at one time to make the $450.00 purchase requirement for 14 grams.

There are 8/16ths in 14 grams or ½ ounce and 1/16 oz. in my normal daily desire of The Juice. $120 per 1/16 is the normal price I pay, plus extra cash for Bones to meet me for the transaction. So, in the math section, 8 purchases of 1/16 + 8 x 120= $960.00, plus fuel, so that's about $960.00 + $48.00 = $1008.00. That's what I would pay over the eight days buying at 1/16 Juice per day. But when I make the large purchase of $450.00 at one time, I get 8 days of Juice for less.

After I make the purchase I separate the ½ ounce into 8 packages of 1/16 and it's at this strategic point we must consider very carefully exactly what the plan is: NOT TO OVERUSE and destroy the savings in the first place. What's happened in the past? Yep, who would have guessed it's so easy to do two 1/16 oz instead of one.

The famous 8-ball or 3 and a half grams is a fat amount of Juice, and every drug addict's dream number but absolutely the wrong technique for any smart user. It's too much to do at once. You can't work effectively, can't eat properly, sleep right, or do anything that normal people do when you've got an 8-ball "rippin" through your veins at lightning speed.

So, we will test Papa Dean's resilience to the drug of choice and fool the system by methodically rationing exactly the correct amount of TNT Juice into my tender system and make a sweet 8-day comfortable journey for myself and all those around me. Working, eating, and sleeping in the correct numbers, even gaining a few pounds in the process.

And I never lie to you or me. And as a reward for my absolute rationing techniques over the entire 8-day period, I will purchase another ½ ounce on the 9th day. The savings will be $558.00.

I know you don't want to be any part of this dumb plan of mine, but are you with me? Even a little? Just with the number concept? Business always comes first, Juice second.

"2012 is a good year to die…this is going to be my year," Dad said. "No way," I told him. "You are like a cockroach, and they survive nuclear wars." "I'm getting tired, Am." Dad replied. Suddenly, I realized the gravity of his statement. The only thing that had kept him going the last few years was his defiant *will* and his "Juice." He was finally succumbing to the inevitable.

Dad's birthday was February 20th. Adam and I wanted to make it a special one. I called Dad and told him that we wanted to celebrate. "Do you want me to plan something at my house, or would you rather us come to yours?" I asked. "It's too hard to travel these days, why don't you come here," he said. "Alright, then it's settled. We will come on Saturday the 18th. Make sure Grandma knows we plan to come and tell her we will bring all the food. She doesn't have to worry about a thing." "Will do," he replied.

A week before the celebration, Dad called and said, "Hey, are you bringing your mom next week? Grandma would like to see her." I told Dad that I mentioned the party to Mom but wasn't sure if she planned to come. *I knew Mom wouldn't miss it.* A day before the celebration, Dad called again. "Bring your mom with you, Grandma wants to see her" he said. "She's coming Dad," I replied, knowing full well *who* really wanted to see her.

Dad must have had so many regrets about Mom. Only two women were capable of the loyalty required to completely subjugate themselves to Dad: Mama Brown and Mom. Come hell or high water, Mom stood fiercely by Dad's side, and in return Dad wiped his ass with her. After the divorce, the one thing Mom repeatedly said, even fifteen years after their relationship ended, was "I am so relieved. I don't have to make excuses for him anymore." Mom didn't have to make excuses anymore, but she would always love Dad, even though he had hurt her so completely.

We ascended the hill to Grandma's house and I honked the horn, just as I always did to signal our arrival. The horn always brought Grandma and Dad outside to the car to greet us, but they didn't come. I went into the house, and Adam was busy making omelets in the kitchen. He had just served one up to Dad, who was seated at the table. "Hey Pops, happy birthday!" I yelled. I went over to give him a hug but was scared to squeeze tightly. He looked so frail.

He had gotten his hair cut for the occasion and had freshly dyed his hair. Dad dyed his own hair, it was pretty obvious. The telltale black stains could be seen on his ears and scalp. I wondered if he was completely gray. He wore a purple button-down shirt, already stained from his omelet, and an old pair of jeans. He couldn't have weighed more than 80 pounds. The bones protruded from his face and his once proud nose lay flat and deflated, eaten away by the cocaine. Dad's dirty set of teeth sat on the table making his cheeks appear particularly concave.

Dad tried to shave that morning but had missed two giant spots below his chin on his neck. I was surprised to see the hair was completely gray. Dried blood was visible on both ears near the top and bottom. He had obviously tried to remove the long hairs that had taken up residence there. Clearly, Dad had gone to great efforts with his appearance; *I suspect it was for Mom.*

I got Dad some of his favorite things for his birthday: an array of different flavored "Schnapps," a boatload of "Junior Mints," and some peanut butter cups. I would have gotten him the "Red Hots" he liked so well, but I didn't think he would be able to chew them. Dad seemed particularly smitten with a book entitled "Useless Information" I selected for him. He read excerpts from it during the visit. I had Mom bring photo albums full of old pictures. I wanted Dad to remember the person he was, handsome and full of life. Dad looked at the pictures and had a grin on his face, but he said little.

The only topic Dad really wanted to discuss was the recent death of Whitney Houston. "Whitney Houston and Michael Jackson just don't know how to do drugs correctly!" He rambled. "I guess I need to do a seminar. I did an "8-ball" of cocaine yesterday and look at me!" *We saw alright, the crypt keeper himself.* None of us were shocked by the statement.

We didn't even bother to scold Dad for talking that way in front of the kids. It just *was what it was,* and Dad had forced us all to completely accept it.

Emphysema was not going to kill Dad…cocaine was. I gave Dad a hug when I left that day and felt the bones in his shoulders and arms. I wondered if this would be the last time I saw him. "You know, I started writing a new book Dad…it's about you." I expected a flash of concern to come over Dad's face, but he smiled a wicked smirk and said, "Am I gonna go to jail?"

A couple of weeks after Dad's birthday celebration, I received a letter from him.

Friday 2nd of March 2012 at 5 am

Howdy Amber,

Hope you're stepping strong! 39 is a lousy year to be at. You're right, 40 is much better, for men anyway. Happy Birthday, My sweet lady! 1973 was a good year. Writing about your Papa Dean are you? A book a comin? What an Honor, what a job!

Lots of "Useless Information" in my head—I read the book you got me a lot. Money for your birthday gift still ranks high up there for me. I've got less coming in without the plumbing business but live very comfortable with Mama B. You and Dean have really done well together, raising two boys is a difficult task, continuous, huh?

Sweet Monday March 5th to ya Am~

Love ya,

Papa Dean

3/7/2012

Dad called a couple days after my birthday and told me he had just been to the doctor. The visit had not gone well. Dad sounded frantic and upset, "I could barely make it into his office from the parking lot. I sucked down a whole tank of oxygen when I got in there." I was surprised Grandma hadn't taken him to the appointment, but quickly remembered how much Dad hated Grandma's driving.

"Listen Am, I just wanted you to know that I have lived exactly how I've wanted. I don't have any fucking regrets." "I know Dad...what's wrong?" "The doctor thinks it's time for hospice. I'm only telling you. You are the only one that can handle it." "Well, what did you tell the doctor Dad?" "I told him to go fuck himself. I'm not going into a hospice!" "Have you been feeling a lot worse?" "I do an eight-ball of cocaine a day. An ounce a week" "Jesus Dad! Are you trying to kill yourself?" "Fuck no, it makes me feel better!"

Dad had been sick for so long, I had just gotten accustomed to his hacking cough and oxygen machines. I hadn't really considered the particulars of "the end." Although I had been preparing for Dad's untimely death since age thirteen, I still felt totally unprepared. Dad had really exceeded his life expectancy considering his lifestyle; I had begun to think he was invincible. I called Grandma that night and talked to her about hospice. She was her upbeat self.

"You know, honey, I volunteered for hospice a few years back. I stopped doing it because I was tired of seeing everyone die. I decided that I still had time to live and needed to do so!" "I know Grandma." "I told your daddy that he may not want hospice, but I do! They can make him comfortable with a bed here at the house and take good care of him. I could really use the help. You know, he smokes around those oxygen tanks. I'm afraid he is going to blow the place up!" "I know Grandma. You could definitely use some help. Well, is Dad ready for hospice?" "When he learned that he could stay here at home to be cared for, he liked that idea. We are going to have hospice come next week." "Well, that's great, Grandma. I'm glad help is on the way."

The following day, I felt compelled to see Dad, so Dean and I took a drive to Grandma's house. I didn't tell Dad we were coming. I wanted to surprise him, but he called my cell phone while we were en route. "Hey Dad, how funny you called! We are on our way to see you!" "Good, see you when you get here," he said before hanging up.

Dad was really happy to see Dean. He hadn't seen him for some time. We visited for a couple of hours and gave Grandma a fire extinguisher to ease her nerves about Dad's smoking. Grandma harped on Dad's smoking around the oxygen tanks much of the visit, which just pissed Dad off. "Shut up!" he sniffed, as he made his way outside to smoke.

When Dean and I got ready to leave, I gave Dad a hug and kissed his cheek. "We'll see you later Dad" I said, knowing deep down that might not happen. "Okay," he said. I walked Grandma out to the car and gave her a long hug. "With this type of care, he is going to stick around for a while and give all those nurses a run for their money" I told Grandma. She and I laughed hysterically thinking about the shenanigans Dad would put those poor volunteers through.

Seeing Dad that day made me realize the importance of saying good-bye. Telling him how much I loved him, despite everything, and coming to a place of peace. So, I sat down and wrote him a letter.

3/9/2012

Hey Pops! I enjoyed our impromptu visit the other day. I plan to pop in to irritate you more often. I'm the only person on Earth who holds you accountable, you made me feisty—probably regretting that now, aren't you?

I have been writing a journal for about two years, detailing my life's journey. You have kept things very exciting over the years. Writing has been very therapeutic for me and gets me in touch with how I'm really feeling. I suspect that is why you also write.

My journal has gained momentum, and I have a new zeal for creative output. I saved letters from you all the way into the 1990's until the present. I enjoyed putting them in order and organizing them. They made me remember how supportive and loving you are and were, in the crazy way only you could deliver.

You are a special human being, truly a one of a kind. Your craziness and reckless abandon does show how much you take life in, and clearly this is why you feel such satisfaction at this point of your journey. Your journey does not end once your shell has resigned. You will be entering a new and wondrous place- as we all soon will.

Take time every day to focus on the beauty of this life. It is all around us. In the flowers, the birds, the water flowing from the fountain, and especially in Grandma—the one woman who loves you so completely and unconditionally. That type of love is rare. Don't return it with ugliness.

Appreciate the love and beauty that surrounds you every day and don't let your "Juice" distract you from that, as it is why God placed us here...to love one another and experience the world in "physical form."

My book will be more about you than me and my journey to interpret a life force such as yours...a POWERFUL one! Use your powers for good and stay in a place of love and gratitude. Don't let things distract you from your purpose...especially now.

I'm thinking about calling the book "Adaptation." Yes, all of your lessons were taught unconventionally. We learned to adapt right around you. But look how strong I am. Thank you! I won't be angry about how the lessons were learned anymore. I will simply be grateful they were learned.

Love you~ Am

3/18/2012

I waited over a week and was surprised when I had not received a letter back from Dad. It was unlike him not to return correspondence. It worried me. I telephoned Dad to see how things were going and was surprised when Grandma answered the phone; Dad always picked up first.

"Hi Grandma, It's Ambie." "Hi sweetie, how are you?" "Fine Grandma. I was calling to see how you guys were getting along." "Well, good. Your daddy is sleeping right now. I'm just waiting for him to get up so I can give him his dinner."

Dad picked up the phone with a groggy "Hello." "Hey Pops! How are ya?" Dad's words came slow and rolled off his tongue as if he were coming out of anesthesia. "What did you say Dad? Jeez, are you abusing the morphine already?" I said half joking.

"What time is it?" Dad asked. "It's five o'clock…dinner time. How long have you been sleeping?" "All night." he replied. "You mean all day?" I asked. "Listen, Dad, did you get my letter?" "Did I ever!" he replied. Dad was out of it, totally sedated, compliments of hospice. Maybe this was best, I wanted him to be comfortable, as did Grandma. "Hey Pops, I'll call you later. You sound tired."

The following day, Mom told me she received a phone call from Dad. "What did he have to say?" I asked. "Amber, I just about fell over. He called to tell me how sorry he was for how he treated me during our marriage. It was so heartfelt and unexpected that I didn't even know what to say." "Well, what *did* you say?" "I told him, it was okay, that it wasn't all that bad because we had fun times too." "Jeez Mom, I would have let him have it! Where is *my* fucking apology?"

3/21/2012

Mom was at my house watching the kids when she got a frantic call from Grandma. Mom called me at work and said, "Call your Grandma, Amber. She called here looking for you. She is upset and crying." "Oh my god, is Dad dead?" "No, he stole your Grandma's car and took off." "What? Jesus, I'll call her!" I called Grandma three times, but no one answered. I called Dad's cell phone and he picked up immediately.

"Talk to me!" He said in a powerful voice.

"Hey Pops, what's going on?"

"Mama took my car keys, so I took hers. I told her to give me my keys back and I would give her hers. She wouldn't, so I took her car. She had no right to take my keys…no right!"

"Dad…."

"I'm having a real rough time. I don't have my oxygen."

"Dad listen, go...."

"Bye."

Dad hung up the phone. Not because he couldn't breathe, but because he knew he wasn't going to like what I was about to say. He refused to accept any responsibility. I waited a few minutes and called back.

"Talk to me!" He said again.

"Dad, go home."

"I told her I would give her keys back if she gave me mine. I told her!" he rambled.

"Dad, aren't you supposed to be on hospice? Where are you going? What do you need so badly that you are willing to get out of your death bed and steal Grandma's car?"

"Bye." He said and hung up again. It was useless.

I called Grandma again, and she picked up the phone. She cried and told me how the day unfolded. Dad woke up that morning and told her, "Why don't you take your ass to the store and get me some cigarettes." Grandma went to the store and returned with Dad's cigarettes. She sat down beside him to talk and he told her, "Go outside and water something, get out of my sight." Grandma said the social worker specifically told her that Dad was under several narcotics, including morphine, and he was prohibited from driving. Grandma said she hid Dad's car keys, so he couldn't leave, and shortly thereafter she discovered Dad and her car were gone.

"Grandma, Dad is going to continue doing what he wants until you disallow it. Don't you see you are holding all of the cards?"

"The social worker told me to call the police, I can't do that!" She cried. "Grandma, you are being held hostage in your own home. You don't have to stand for it. Tell Dad to leave!"

"Where would he go?"

"He has disability money. We can threaten to put him in a convalescent hospital."

"I can't do that. He wouldn't last two months at a place like that."

"Grandma, he is one step from death anyway. He has no quality of life, and he wants to take that out on you. He isn't going to stop. Tell him he has to leave if he is going to continue to act this way; Grandma, he is killing you!"

"Well, I'm 88 anyway."

I didn't want Dad to spend his last days at some hospital. I just figured Grandma could threaten to kick him out and maybe he would behave.

"Grandma, how long are you going to wait to call the police? How long has he been gone?" I asked.

"About an hour and a half." She replied.

"He can't be gone that long. He doesn't have his oxygen. Are you sure he didn't creep back into the house without you knowing?" I asked.

"Hang on. Let me go check to see if my car is in the driveway. Oh… wait, he's back. I see my car! It's parked right behind his van. I'm so glad. I hope he is okay. I'm going to go sweetie. I will try to be strong with him."

Grandma was no match for Dad. Dad was sure to kill her. I called Adam to tell him what was going on. "Did you hear from Dad, Adam?"

"Ya, he left me a message."

"What did he say?" I asked.

"He said, 'Your sister told Grandma to call the cops on me...she's a rat!'"

Shit, Grandma told Dad what I said. I didn't dare call the house. I would wait till things cooled off. Nine days later...they did.

CHAPTER 25

Free Bird

3/30/2012

Dad died on a Friday. The sky was gray, and it was cold when I returned home from my walk. Mom was waiting for me at my house with tears in her eyes. "Mom, what's wrong?" "I've got some bad news…your Dad died this morning." I stood there with a blank expression…as if surprised. I had been preparing for this moment since I was thirteen. How could I possibly be shocked? Turns out, no amount of preparation was enough. I walked up the stairs, held Mom, and cried like a baby. Long blubbering sobs that told a story of profound heartbreak.

Mom and I headed out to Grandma's house. We sat in silence as I drove and after a while, Mom started laughing.

"You know what my last words were to your father?"

"What?" I asked.

"Fuck you!" Mom started laughing again.

"Oh God that's right, I forgot about that," I said.

Mom told me days earlier that she called Dad to scold him for stealing Grandma's car. "How can you treat your mother this way?" She lectured. "I don't want to hear it! I'm going to hang up on you" Dad threatened. Mom wouldn't let Dad have the last word. She was furious with him and yelled, "I'll hang up on you…Fuck you!" Mom said she had never felt more satisfaction from hanging up on someone. Mom never stood up to Dad like that. It must have felt good.

"Should I stop and pick up food Mom?"

"That's a good idea," Mom replied.

"Costco is at the bottom of the hill. I'll stop there and get some flowers too. You can just wait in the car," I told Mom.

I walked into Costco like a robot. I passed by the carts deciding I had no need for one and as I was heading back to the bakery, I saw avocado trees for sale. *Yes, a tree* I thought…*we'll plant one today.* I grabbed the heavy pot and headed back for the muffins. Then I stood there a long while wondering how I would carry everything back to the register. The tree really required two hands. *Christ…maybe I shouldn't get the tree, what was I thinking anyway? Flowers were more practical…I could just leave the tree sit there abandoned in the aisle. Someone would put it back.*

I stood there for a while contemplating my dilemma. I certainly wasn't going to go all the way back to the front of the store for a cart, and I was not leaving without that tree. I would just have to carry it all. *Impractical; I am my father's daughter*, I thought. I grabbed two packs of muffins in one arm and held the tree in the other. I walked briskly to the register but had to stop three times to set the tree down when I thought I might drop it. Finally, I made it to the register, where a man put it all in a cart for me. As I left the store, the woman at the door checking my receipt said, "Well, you got an avocado tree! If you're lucky, you might have an avocado next year."

I took the receipt and cried as I walked to the car thinking, *Dad would have found someone to carry that fucking tree to the register for him.* He was masterful when it came to delegating his needs. I don't know how he did it, but Dad had a way of making people actually feel grateful to be at his service.

When we got to Grandma's house several relatives had already gathered there. I hugged Grandma for a long time and cried. "Honey, it's okay. He lived such a good life. He had no regrets," she told me. "I know Grandma," I sobbed. Grandma put her arms around me and walked me toward the hallway. "The hospice nurse said that he didn't fall, he just laid down in the hallway and went to sleep." We rounded the corner, and Dad lay there in a fetal position. A shock immediately set in. *Dad was still here?* It had been hours since Grandma called Mom, why hadn't someone from hospice come to collect him? I frantically looked around for Mom. She couldn't see this! She couldn't handle it! "Hospice came this morning to get your daddy, but I wanted everyone to get to see him, so they could say goodbye," Grandma explained.

God give me strength, I thought to myself, as I stood there looking at Dad's lifeless body. "Mom, don't come over here...." Mom rounded the corner as the words came out of my mouth. She looked down, and her eyes grew wide with panic. "Oh my God, he's still here!" she wailed, as she backed away.

I went over and knelt beside Dad. He lay there quiet, peaceful. He was already dressed for the day, wearing his jeans and the familiar stained dinner jacket. He still wore his glasses and an inhaler lay in his hand. I placed my hand on Dad's hard back and ran my hand over his hair. *It had lost its shine.* His skinny little body had endured so much, more than humanly possible. His *will* had kept him alive at the end. I wondered why he chose the hallway for his final resting place. Did he want his death to be obvious for Grandma? Was he afraid that she would think he was asleep if he were in his bed? I was convinced that everything was of Dad's choosing; death was no different. I cried and held his cold hand ...*goodbye daddy.*

Dad lay in the hallway for hours until two young men from a funeral home finally came to collect him. "Oh, they are here to take Dean!" Grandma wailed. She headed down the hallway and cradled Dad in her arms for a long time. She sobbed, and my heart ached knowing how painfully unnatural it must feel to lose a child. I don't think Grandma left Dad there in the hallway for us to say goodbye. She wasn't ready to let go, and the thought of physically parting with him was too much to bear. If she were allowed, I think Grandma would have held on to Dad's empty shell until it putrefied. The young man stumbled through some questions with Adam, and then he and his coworker rolled the gurney down the hall. *What a job…*I thought.

I retreated to the patio and then came back toward the hall. "You don't want to see this part Am, stay here." Adam said. Adam and I backed away and waited for the gurney to emerge from around the corner. A few minutes later, the young man appeared with something in his hand. "This was in his pocket," he said. But the look on his face said it all. I knew exactly what the young man was holding. My uncle walked over to collect the item as Adam briskly followed behind. *Adam knew too.* "Give it to my brother," I told the young man in a stern voice and my uncle retreated.

The man discretely gave my brother the contents of Dad's pockets, a baggie of cocaine and a stack of $100.00 bills. It was pretty evident that had Dad's *"Plan A"* failed to pan out; he was moving to *"Plan B"*…and I'm pretty certain that involved stealing Grandma's car again. Adam took the money, set it down on the table, and slid the cocaine discreetly in his pocket.

We stayed with Grandma until dark and told stories about Dad. Mom told Grandma how badly she felt about her last words to Dad. Grandma told Mom, "Oh honey, don't feel bad. When he got off the phone he said, 'that bitch hung up on me…I'm proud of her.'" Dad could always appreciate acts of defiance. Much of the time, defiant acts coming from someone other than himself gave him equal satisfaction.

I was the person who resisted Dad the most and strangely, I was also the person most similar to him. I think that is why Dad handled me the way he did. He never seemed to take it personally, which just pissed me off. I think he admired my fight too much to condemn it. *I reminded him of him.*

We planted the avocado tree in the backyard close to the edge of the hill overlooking the entire valley. *How wonderfully fitting, King of the fucking hill,* I thought. Grandma picked the spot, and I dug the hole. Adam, Becky, and my cousin stood and watched as I placed the little tree in the ground and covered it with dirt. Grandma dedicated the tree to Dad and urged it to grow big, strong, and full of fruit. My cousin Erin then said, "You know, your Dad would have much rather we planted a marijuana tree." We all laughed, contemplating how much Dad would have appreciated that act of defiance.

Dad wrote down everything, even stuff that made no sense…disjointed thoughts, stories, but mostly plans. He had a penchant for writing and communicated best through this medium. I suspect it was therapeutic for him, just as it is for me. We found a stack of papers with the cremation paperwork. Dad diligently detailed and chronicled his wishes and thoughts.

3/23/2012: I want to be in charge of my own medication. I have three categories of meds. Plus air bottles and "E" type tanks. I keep exact records, maintain supplies, levels, and secure ordering of all meds. Morphine, Percoset, Acetaminophen, Spiriva, Q-var, Albuterol, Bisac, Lorazepam, Zolpidem.

3/24/2012: Personal: When it becomes more difficult to live than to let go, it's time to enter the next domain. I have certainly arrived at this TURNOUT and have earned my right to take it as I see fit. No loose ends and no fear of death will make my trip much easier to enter.

3/24/2012: Ongoing issues. Shorted buy yesterday 3/23/2012. Bought half ounce of juice and only got six grams. I called Poncho and told him that

I was shorted. I asked him to tell Zovia that I was aware of the discrepancy and will wait for it to be corrected. I have been a very loyal and consistent customer for many years and never let them down or shorted them money. I deserve the absolute BEST treatment and expect it.

3/28/2012: I signed a "Pull the plug" statement. NO RESUSCITATION! Yep, that's right "Big Dog" has spoken, therefore we will all be happy. So, let it be- Dino

Dad's last entry was the day before he died.

3/29/2012: To whoever comes in. Surprise visit from hospice RN (Matt). We all three spoke to each other to get an exact evaluation of our living conditions including the meds (legal and illegal) taken and medical risks of making the correct decision. You with me? I certainly hope so. What a relief for ME to have all Matt's position of authority should there be any outside attempts to take over. Both son and daughter have partial knowledge of my health condition. Matt needs to talk to both to relax their need to take over. Ain't quite yet, but close to cooking my butt.

The spirit of Papa Dean will live on! I dedicate my "spirits" to my sweet family. Through Adam, Amber, AJ, Brandon, Conner, Carson, and especially Dean and Debra will carry my spirit forever and that I am very sure of! I am very pleased to have chosen the cremation process for my spirit and soul; it's the right way for me, 100%. Be pleased that these are my loving wishes and take a lot of comfort in this most natural completion of life. I should go out with a lot of FIRE. Don't you all agree! I loved every minute of life and regret nothing. Few people have accomplished as much as I have or experienced as many hits as I have.

If I could, I'd have Adam pour half the ashes around the tree in the driveway. We call it the "Spirit of Dad Brown." You know which one, Adam. Sure, it's against the law to do that, what a surprise that I ask this of you. Dispose of the rest of the ashes on ground you like…only we will know. My spirit is not in my ash! It is in your heart.

You are all a fine family and I am most pleased to have felt each of your love for me and NO man could ask for more! Kick Ass each and every one of you and know that I sure did…and loved it. Go for it! Love ya, Papa Dean

I am quite certain that Dad planned every detail of his departure. He intended to use his *"medication"* and *"take his turnout"* as he saw fit. Dad always told me, "Make your own plans…or be at the mercy of those who make them for you." Until the very end, life and even death would be on Dad's terms. Adam and I found letters Dad had written to us a couple of years earlier. I never asked to read Adam's letter; I didn't need to.

To Amber, You made it very "sweet" for me Amber. Your acceptance was most pleasing. You have the same "gene pool" from the get. I've learned more from you in the last twenty years than anyone would expect…what a prize you've been for me. Love you all and know you will go forth with strength and compassion.

Papa Dean

Adam held me, and I sobbed. "It's okay Am" he reassured me, a way a father might. I instantly thought of Mom all those years ago. The way she sought Adam's comfort when Dad disappeared for days at a time to gamble. Adam was the rock, the constant that kept Mom sane and gave Dad prideful purpose. Adam was the calm in our family's storm, the compass that drove us into the steady places.

Everyone said that Adam looked just like "an old man" when he was born. I like to believe he was an old soul brought to earth to impart lessons to my parents. My folks had more life experience, but Adam had true spiritual maturity. Adam's patient acceptance of Dad was nothing short of remarkable. Even into adulthood, when we actually had a choice to disagree with Dad and reject his behavior, Adam's dedication to Dad's wishes remained unfaltering and without judgment.

I called Adam many times to air my frustrations. I condemned Dad's behavior in search of an ally to commiserate the perverted injustices, but Adam never sided with my condemnation. I was unwilling to accept Dad's choice to self-destruct. It was too hurtful. Adam somehow managed an unassuming, unconditional love and totally accepted Dad... a man who tested the limits of human forgiveness.

I was swept with a sadness knowing my and Adam's burden. We had to make so many difficult decisions and grow up so fast. It really was a miracle we'd turned out so well. I had spent a good portion of my life trying to "catch up" to Adam, to fill in my perceived inadequacies and rival him. But at that moment, I knew Adam played a role in our family that could be filled by no other. Each of us had a role to play in our family, and those roles made us who we are. I owe my fighting strength mostly to Dad. He was my biggest saboteur but also my greatest teacher, and for that I am thankful.

I believe our life's course is our own choosing. Before we are even in physical form, we decide our lessons. Some pick charmed paths and enjoy life's finer offerings, while others choose challenging destinies, fated for hardship but also for absolute growth and greatness. Adam and I chose hardship and greatness. I wondered if Adam knew how successful our journeys were.

CHAPTER 26

The Hawk

Adam called Ken and Anne the day after Dad died. They were Dad's most treasured living friends. They lived back East, in Georgia I think, and he wrote to them nearly every day. Ken and Anne were two of the most conservative people on earth, such an odd combination to be paired with Dad. Dad was so predictably zany that only the brave could keep him close. Indeed, Ken and Anne were a courageous couple. *Dad was such a loyal friend.*

Ken was heartbroken when he learned Dad had died. "We planned to come to Los Angles at the end of May. We were going to surprise him. I bet he would have hung on had he known that. Hold on Adam, I need to pull over and have a good cry." Adam filled Ken in on the details, and Ken shared a story with Adam that neither he nor I had ever heard.

You know, we met your parents on that cruise years and years ago. We were paired with them at dinner time with a couple of other people. The night before the cruise was over, your Dad made a bet with one of the guys at our table that he would be the first one off the ship the following morning. The guy scoffed and doubted Dad. They shook hands on their fifty-dollar wager and that night, the guy packed up his belongings, found out which door the passengers would be let off, and was the first in line to depart. He actually planned to sleep there in line to win that bet. Your Dad walked by him at one point, and that guy laughed at him and said, "Hey, get ready to pony up that fifty bucks."

The next morning, the ship docked, and the guy was pretty satisfied knowing he was first in line to depart; surely, he would collect the fifty dollars. But when the doors opened and that guy stepped out, there stood your Dad… all wet. He had somehow managed to jump off the ship and swim back to the dock before they even opened the ship's doors.

Jesus, that was my Dad. He was a force.

Dad didn't want a funeral. He left specific instructions detailing his wishes, "I'd rather have a celebration of life party with alcohol, drugs, and smoking if possible. I lived on the edge of life whenever possible. If you aren't living on the edge, then you are taking up too much space." I wanted to send Dad off right. He savored every moment of life; maybe he was one of the few who truly realize how fleeting it is.

Dad made it pretty easy. I found a hand-written note in his belongings entitled, "Call these people." The list of friends was numbered, but Dad had instructions to tell each they were "first on the list." I sat down and began calling Dad's friends, a collection of underdogs…just like him. Each told a story or two about Dad, and many told me he was "the craziest guy they knew." Some of the stories were familiar, but many I had never heard. Dad was wild beyond calculation. Everything he did was a wild story to tell…I wish I knew all his stories.

The thing that struck me as I talked to each of Dad's friends was the odd feeling of familiarity. It was as if each of Dad's friends knew me, even though we had never met. *I was obviously one of Dad's favorite topics.* At the end of each conversation, Dad's friends told me the same thing, "Amber, he was so proud of you." I knew Dad was proud of me. Why then didn't I feel like a *prize*, as he had written in his note to me? Clearly, everyone else knew this to be true…but me.

Dad's celebration took place in my backyard. Tables draped in dark purple linen and bouquets of red roses lined the yard. I hung bird cages adorned with red roses from garden umbrellas and opened each cage door. Dad was finally free, a *Free Bird*. Dad was loved and his friends were loyal. Even his tax preparer showed up. He told me, "I've been doing your Dad's taxes for years. The first time we met, he showed up at my office with a briefcase containing his tax paperwork and a gun. I just about died."

Dad's party was a true celebration of life—alcohol, cigarettes, street tacos, music, dancing, pictures, and stories…lots and lots of stories. At the end of the day, a poem was read, and we released one hundred red and purple balloons. I released two balloons for Dad and as they left my hands, I was struck by the beauty of their liberation, the way they danced so peacefully with the wind into the heavens and beyond sight.

The Journey

Purple and red balloons abound

They ascend to the heavens and leave the ground

Like me they will have floated on Earth for a time

To enjoy God's beauty before making the climb

Release this balloon as you have released my shell

And send it in love to the place where I dwell

I will wait and collect them one by one

And will be holding them waiting for your time to be done

Do not be sad, for my soul has been freed

God and his angels have been waiting in need

I learned all my lessons in physical form

Now have deeds and God's work to perform

I love you all and don't worry about life's close

For it is just the beginning and where God's love flows

Look deep, my spirit is locked in your heart

Along with God's while we wait a moment apart

Perspective is a strange thing…it can totally differ among people and yet be accurate for each one. A contradiction of realities in which neither party can claim correctness. I spent the better half of my life trying to change others around me, especially Dad. And when saving Dad wasn't enough, I sought out opportunities to fulfill this exercise in futility elsewhere: rotten boyfriends, lousy friends, even my career. I tried to save them all, and none of them wanted saving. *None of them thought they needed saving.*

Accepting Dad's happiness proved tiring and frustrating, but not as futile as trying to disprove it. Every time I thought I had come to accept Dad, he'd behave deplorably yet again. I perceived each act as a personal affront, but it was nothing personal. Change can only come from within, not from without, and I had spent the bulk of my time attempting to change destinies that did not belong to me. Dad was perfectly happy with his life and the outcome of his choices; *it was I who rejected it.*

One moment I accepted Dad's behavior because I knew it would never change, but the next moment I loathed and rejected it. This cycle repeated itself over and over throughout the years and became particularly unbearable during my adult years. The ambivalence was maddening, and my past seemed insurmountable. Then I discovered the problem. *Did Dad love me?*

I gave this thought considerable time to stew and was surprised I hadn't pinpointed the primary issue: *my uncertainty of being loved.* Dad's behavior left this issue up *for perceptual debate.* Only I could answer the question that truly plagued me, and it would come from a deeper place, not from analyzing Dad's behavior. I rejected the way Dad demonstrated love—the only way in which he was capable. I chose not to believe in his love and focused on the faults that masked the good in him. I did not want Dad to be a drug addict. I did not understand or accept his path. I loved Dad so much that I could not allow him *to be* and experience his journey. I disagreed with it and had unwittingly placed conditions on my love; something Dad was incapable of doing with me. I could have been an utter failure "a hooker with crabs" as Dad always joked, and his love for me would not have wavered. Why hadn't I accepted this truth?

Everyone has their own reality. My reality certainly did not mirror Dad's, but in the end, I finally concluded this …you cannot assume to know what is best for someone else or they for you. Dad's journey was his own, just as mine is my own. I think everyone comes to find *The Divine* differently; no matter what the path, we all arrive at the same place, Love, and Dad had so much in his heart.

Dad lived wild and free, as only a young soul can. My old soul could not influence or confine his spirit. *It wasn't supposed to.* Dad lived with the type of abandon few will ever experience. His spirit had a gravitational pull that attracted all and lives in me. Written, unwritten, unspoken, you are forgiven Dad. *Yes, he loved me completely, there is no doubt.*

Eulogy for my Father

My Dad was something of an enigma…a fictional character frolicking through life gobbling it up like "Pac Man." He was spontaneous, daring, inspiring, charismatic…and very hard to kill. He spit in death's eye numerous times, and I know he left this Earth on his own terms…when he was darned good and ready!

We have all had the privilege of knowing my Dad in our respective relationships…he was a son, a brother, a father, a husband, a cousin, and a friend. The remarkable thing is, we all knew the same Dean…he did not change his behavior to fit any stereotype or role expectation. He was transparent, unadulterated, full strength, and uniquely genuine in all his relationships. Dad was "dreadfully honest." He would tell you if you were overweight, if you smelled, if he didn't like your outfit. His honesty sometimes stung, but truly, this is one of the traits that endeared him to us all. He was a straight shooter incapable of sugar-coating anything. If I wanted a truthful opinion, Dad was my man.

My Dad was fearless. "Try everything once Amber," he told me. He followed his own advice and constantly embarked on new territory. His potential was astounding. He really was brilliant. He managed to build a successful printing shop in his early 20's and when he tired of that, he bull-shitted his way into the aerospace industry and built fighter jets and space shuttles. In the interim, he went back to school and earned a Master's degree from Pepperdine University. His thesis detailed the tooling process in the aerospace industry.

After that, Dad decided to tackle the plumbing business, which he knew absolutely nothing about. He learned the trade, got licensed, and then in true trail blazer style he started his own business. Dad got such enjoyment helping the new people he met. He operated his plumbing business until the very end and took such pleasure in passing the baton to his good friend Frankie.

Dad was a champion of underdogs. I think because he fancied himself one. Throughout his life, he sought out people who could use a break...then did what he could to help them out. He had a huge heart and loved to surprise and entertain people. He gave the term "comic relief" new meaning and showed us all a more playful side to life. Either through his antics or his gestures, Dad would break into your heart...and you would hold him there, despite the fact that he was so misbehaved.

Being raised by such a free-spirited man posed some serious challenges. None of Dad's lessons were taught conventionally, and sometimes this frustrated me. But ultimately, these opportunities only proved to make me stronger. I am my father's daughter, independent, fearless, a fighter...just like him.

I have so many stories about my Dad. I could stand here all day and make you laugh and even cry detailing his life…but you will have to wait for the book. Dad knew I was writing a book largely about him. I told him a couple of months before he died. You know what he said when he found out? "Am I going to go to jail?" I thought that was pretty funny, but my Grandma's comment really made me laugh. She said, "Honey, the book will have to be in the fiction section, because nobody would ever believe it!" So true….

The day my Dad died, I sat in the yard he shared with my Grandma and listened to the quiet. I looked up and saw a hawk circling overhead…strong and powerful. Four days later, I went back to Dad's house and packed up his things. While we were there, Adam and I went to visit the avocado tree we planted in Dad's honor. Adam threw a cigarette butt near the tree, and said, "Thrive bitch." Dad would have really appreciated that. We looked overhead and a hawk circled the little tree and us. "Do you think that's Dad Adam?" "Yeah, he's watching us like a hawk," he replied. Strange, as the days passed, everywhere I looked, I saw another hawk….

Dad asked that his ashes be spread on the tree that sprouted through the asphalt at Grandma's house after my Grandpa Cecil died. We lovingly call it, "The Cecil Tree," and my Grandma has decorated its trunk with a face and a sailor hat. Dad also has his own tree now, and his ashes will be spread there too. For those of you who like to visit the memorial of loved ones who have transcended to their next journey, there is no need. My Dad's spirit lives in all your hearts…and the next time you see a hawk, think of him and know that he is watching over you too.

CHAPTER 27

Final Chapter

Shortly after Dad died, in 2012, I finished writing *Free Bird*. I had friends and family read my manuscript and for reasons unknown to me then, I "shelved" my project, and my story sat on a flash drive in my kitchen's silverware drawer. I guess I wasn't ready to serve up (pun intended) the history, people, and events that have shaped *who I am*. Frankly, after letting some people read my story, I felt a strange vulnerability. A couple of my friends who had never met Dad seemed upset. They returned my manuscript with that look on their face...like they had just swallowed a bitter pill. One friend even told me, "Your Dad was an *asshole*, I'm mad at him." I couldn't help but feel I had villainized Dad, and certainly I did not want people's takeaway of him to be so negative. Was I unable to capture his essence? The part of him that was inspiring and charismatic? Dad probably wouldn't have cared what people thought of him anyway. He would have been pleased as punch to be a lead character in any book. My best friend Becky, who incidentally found her calling as a talented medium and Reiki healer, read the manuscript and knew Dad well. She told me the book was riveting but wasn't finished. She also told me that I was going to go through something very difficult, but it was going to be life changing and would be the missing piece to my book.

Go through something indeed. In 2016, something did happen. I left my job...or rather, my job left me. After nearly twenty years working in corrections as a probation officer, what I believed to be my life's purpose and work, things came to a screeching halt. In a nutshell, it went down like this...I'm at a meeting with my peers, my boss, and my boss's boss. The big boss is there to find out how the new programs were going, and he asked for our feedback. I launched into a dissertation of what I truly believed to be ground-breaking information. I passionately highlighted the current problems in the system and gave solutions to what I thought could tackle delinquency in the youthful offenders we supervised under probation. The big boss looked me square in the eyes and replied, "Your philosophy is inconsistent with the department's and you should transfer."

Now, without going into the back stories and depth of the injustices perpetrated by an apathetic government agency (maybe that will be my next book) suffice it to say, this comment represented the "straw that broke the camel's back." I somehow managed to wait the five minutes until the meeting concluded before exploding into tears. This marked my last day as a juvenile probation officer and the beginning of a deep depression. A complete emotional and physical breakdown. My health deteriorated, and I believed my life's work, my very purpose here on Earth was over. I suffered over three years, and finally conceded to the end of my career and subsequent retirement.

Then one day it happened. Something just clicked, and I realized that *loss* is sometimes a beautiful gift. Every type of loss in my life has served in some type of growth. The loss of my innocence, childhood, father, and career had ultimately brought me closer to the truth. My life's work is ME. We get lost in our mission to discover self-love and become susceptible to distraction and self-destructive behavior. The meaning of our lives becomes unclear, and the frustration we feel gives way to confusion and chaos. We feel unfulfilled and rudderless, unable to identify the *void*. We lose our way to our true mission here on earth -- *Self-love*. I constantly gave the power to love myself away to others. If they valued me, loved me, found me worthy and good, then in fact, I was all those things. I looked to my father to validate me. I looked to my deeds and service to others for my fulfillment. I even looked to shitty management at a government job to SHOW ME MY WORTH. I came away knowing the truth and as far as I'm concerned, the very meaning of life. We are here on earth to learn love, more specifically self-love, which naturally gives way to the ability to love all other things. This lesson visits each of us a million different ways, but I suspect the lesson is never an easy one. Why do we find ourselves so unlovable? If you think about it, humans find the most torturous ways to subconsciously self-destruct…putting poison into our bodies, starving ourselves, gorging ourselves, cutting ourselves, allowing ourselves to be abused by others, losing control of our very *will* through all types of addictions or the most extreme example- ending it all and taking one's own life. Why?

I simply cannot explain this human condition, the tendency to want to beat ourselves up, but I believe self-love is the key that will end all human suffering. Love is more than an emotion, it is a powerful *drive* necessary for survival. Just as we are driven to eat or reproduce, so too are we driven to find love. When we truly learn to love and accept ourselves and no longer look to others to fulfill this human need, we will finally stumble upon the *Divine*, that piece of God that resides in each of us. Then, we will truly know peace and contentment…like I feel right at this very moment.

In loving memory of my sweet Grandma Brown

1924-2018